Theodor Leschetizky

The Leschetizky Method

A Guide to Fine and Correct Piano Playing

Malwine Brée

English translation by
Arthur Elson

Introduction by
Seymour Bernstein

DOVER PUBLICATIONS, INC.
Mineola, New York

Bibliographical Note

This Dover edition, first published in 1997, is a slightly revised and reordered but otherwise unabridged republication of *The Leschetizky Method: An Exposition of His Personal Views / Published with his approval by his assistant Malwine Brée / With forty-seven illustrations of Leschetizky's hand / The only genuine and authorized treatise explanatory of the Leschetizky method of teaching / A Guide to Fine and Correct Piano Playing / Translated by Arthur Elson*, originally published by The University Society Inc., New York, 1913—an edition, but with new supplementary articles, translated in 1902 from *Die Grundlage der Methode Leschetizky . . .* , originally published by B. Schott's Söhne, Mainz, 1902 (4th ed., 1914).

The Dover edition borrows Leschetizky's photograph from the German edition, as frontispiece, and adds an introduction by Seymour Bernstein written specially for this edition. Three supplementary articles included in the 1913 English edition but absent from the German have been retained: "Exercises Without Keyboard" by Clement Antrobus Harris, "Other Piano Methods" by Arthur Elson and "Practical Hints on Piano Study" by Ignace J. Paderewski (a Leschetizky disciple). A portion of Elson's article—"Time Tables for Practice"—has been deleted along with "Paderewski," a short article by T. P. Currier, both portions considered by the publisher to be less significant in context. The photographs of Leschetizky's hand are taken from the German edition, replacing the somewhat inferior reproductions of the English version.

International Standard Book Number: 0-486-29596-6

Manufactured in the United States of America
Dover Publications, Inc., 31 East 2nd Street, Mineola, N.Y. 11501

TABLE OF CONTENTS

Introduction to the Dover Edition

Of the many well-known pedagogues in the performing arts, few have so profoundly influenced their pupils as did Theodor Leschetizky. A student of Carl Czerny, he, and therefore all of his pedagogical descendants, were related to Beethoven himself.

According to anecdotes told to me by two of my own teachers—Clara Husserl and Alexander Brailowsky, both disciples of Leschetizky—the master's chief asset lay not in methodology but in his uncanny ability to adapt his teaching to the needs of each pupil: "I am in principle no friend of theoretical piano methods," he responded to his former student Malwine Brée. One might say, then, that the only piano method worthy of perpetuating Leschetizky's genius is no fixed method at all—a point supported by Brée in her introductory letter to this publication: "This work is not intended as an over-zealous insistence on the letter of the law, but is meant to be a guide to correct and beautiful playing."

We know, and Brée reiterates, that no method or guide can lead to artistic mastery. For teachers and students who oppose dry finger exercises, keep in mind that it is not *what* you practice that is important, but rather *how* you practice. Since Leschetizky was imbued with the deepest musicality, all of the exercises in this book must be played musically, with carefully controlled dynamics and an even pulse. A key to this is Brée's precise dynamics for the practice of the C major scales (page 18). One can even skip the exercises in favor of such important reminders as "The ear is the guide, and the student must be able to hear . . . any undesired inequality . . ." (page 7), and on the calming effect of her remarks on our fingers' natural interdependency (page 11). We are reminded, too, to stay close to the front of the keys where the key descent is deepest, and to use smaller, more economical motions when playing fast passages.

While Leschetizky had set ideas about physicality at the keyboard—ideas which have found their way into this book—he was opposed to the pursuit of technical perfection for its own sake. So when Alexander Brailowsky once said to me at a lesson that "tone is an expression of your soul," he perhaps summed up his own teacher's philosophy. In fact, when teaching, Leschetizky might well have changed his favorite motto—"No life without art, no art without life"—to "No technique without musicality, no musicality without technique."

Seymour Bernstein
New York, Fall 1996

Pianist, master teacher, composer and writer, Seymour Bernstein studied with Alexander Brailowsky, Nadia Boulanger, George Enescu, Sir Clifford Curzon and Jan Gorbaty. He has performed and lectured worldwide. His book *With Your Own Two Hands* is required reading in conservatories and colleges in this country and abroad, and his publications for piano study have been hailed as "firsts of their kind" and "landmarks in music education."

To my Honored Master,
PROFESSOR THEODOR LESCHETIZKY.

Twenty years have gone since I had the honor of being your pupil, and more than ten since you held me worthy of being your assistant. I mention this to you as justification for holding myself qualified to make public in this book what you taught me during all this time, and what I have proved by hundreds of pupils.

I recognize that a theoretical treatise can no more make a finished pianist than books on painting or sculpture can make a painter or sculptor. But my book may still have its excuse for existence; many older pupils of the Leschetizky school will find it a welcome reminder of what they have learned, while for the younger ones it will give a clear exposition of the principles of the school.

I have tried in this book to avoid all pedantry. This work is not intended as an overzealous insistence on the letter of the law, but is meant to be a guide to correct and beautiful playing. I hope it will succeed in this, if only to merit the distinction given to it by the pictures of your hand.

I thank you most cordially for those, and ask you to accept the dedication of my book. It will thus give homage to the source from which we all have drawn our inspiration.

Most Respectfully,
MALWINE BRÉE.

Vienna, February 1902

Mme. Dr. Malwine Brée,
HONORED MADAME:

Please accept my best thanks for the dedication of your book, which I naturally accept most gladly. As you know, I am in principle no friend of theoretical piano methods; but your excellent work, which I have read through carefully, expresses my personal views so strikingly that I subscribe to everything in it, word for word. Your "Basis of the Leschetizky Method" leads with skilful hand along the same path by which you, as my assistant, have for so many years reached your brilliant successes. Also the style of your work is not merely didactic, but enlivened by intellect and humor. I recognize the pictures of my hand as correct and good; and I wish for your book which I declare the only correct description of my school and method, the best success and the widest publicity.

Yours most Respectfully,
THEODOR LESCHETIZKY.

Vienna, February 24, 1902

THE BASIS OF THE LESCHETIZKY METHOD

I. Attitude at the Piano

ESCHETIZKY used to say, "Sit easy and erect at the piano, like a good rider on his horse, and yield to the arm movements, as far as needed, just as the horseman yields to the movements of his steed." One should sit far enough from the keyboard to let the finger-tips rest on the keys without effort when the arms are normally bent, and the feet reach the pedals without stretching. The elbows should not be consciously pressed against the sides, nor should they be moved away from the sides, as a rule; and they should be kept either on a level with the keys or very slightly above them. Owing to the weaker leverage, too low a seat will cause increased exertion in performance, so that the player is forced to raise his shoulders in very ungraceful fashion when trying to use any power.

Many eminent artists place too little stress on a graceful position at the keyboard. They seem to think it enough if the ear is satisfied. But it surely does no harm to influence the listener's ear through his eye, and make the former more receptive.

"Posing" is not to be approved. The poseur's usual method is to lean back with an air of being inspired, and to play with the head waving about and the eyes cast upward in rapt gaze. Then there is the careless pose of disdainful ease; or the pianist buries his head in the keys, raising it in pauses to give the audience a questioning smile.

Such procedure makes a more or less comic effect, and will detract from the impression of the best performance. Real feeling in piano-playing is not expressed by an emotional pose. The performer's art is shown by his fingers, not his face; and if the player has real feeling, it will display itself naturally.

II. Position of the Hand

The pianist will have little use for a super-refined hand, with slender shape and well-kept nails. A well-trained piano hand is broad, flexible in the wrist, equipped with wide finger-tips, and muscular. The nails must be kept well trimmed, for the elastic finger-tip gives a richer tone than the hard nail.

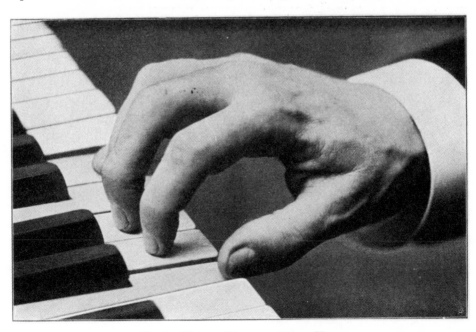

Fig. 1.—How to Hold the Right Hand.

Very large hands are not always a great help to the pianist; but very small ones are usually a disadvantage, even though they are more adapted to bear fatigue, or to acquire the "pearly touch." Large hands have the advantage in dealing with wide intervals or chords, for which small hands must use rapid skips or some other suitable device. As a matter of fact, there have been great pianists with large hands, and others with small hands. The method of holding the hands is the same in either case. The hand

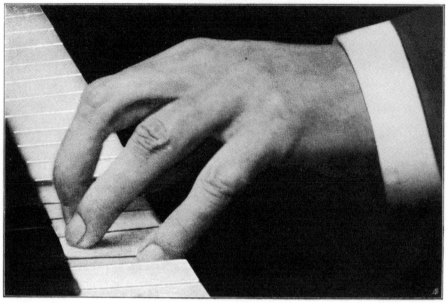

FIG. 2.—HOW TO HOLD THE LEFT HAND.

should be given a noticeably arched shape (see Fig. 1 and Fig. 2); for the rounding of the hand is the only way to get full strength in the finger-attack. Flat hands and fingers give an amateurish effect. The wrist should be held a trifle lower than the knuckles. Only the tips of the fingers are to touch the keys, and the fingers must be curved in such a way that the tip-joints are held vertically. The thumb is an exception, and strikes the key with its side edge, near the tip. The thumb is held away from the fingers, with its tip-joint bent a little.

The fingers should now be set on five adjacent white keys, and all (including the thumb) pressed down together. They are to be kept near the front of the keys, where the touch is lightest, but not so near

FIG. 3.

as to be in danger of slipping off. As the fingers are of unequal length, their tips will form a curve, with the middle finger nearest the black keys.

[EDITOR'S NOTE.—It will be found that each hand has a tendency to lean over outward, the right hand to the right side, and the left hand to the left side. This tendency may be counteracted by letting each hand skip a note between the second and third fingers, instead of having each hand press down five adjacent notes. The right hand will thus take C, D, F, G, and A, while the left hand, from the thumb downward, will use the notes A, G, E, D, and C. By practising some of the exercises in this way, as well as on adjacent notes, the student will soon gain control over the position of the hand.]

III. EXERCISE FOR THE WRIST

As soon as the position of the hand is well under control, press the fingers rather firmly on the five white keys, then raise and lower the wrist slowly several times, keeping the fingers on the keys. In this exercise take good care that (1) the hand keeps its rounded shape, (2) the fingers do not slide on the keys, (3) the wrist does not ever rise above its original position, and (4) the upper arm is moved as little as possible. Each hand is to be taken by itself, and the hands alternated to avoid undue effort. The exercise may be repeated frequently. (See Fig. 3.)

IV. SOME GENERAL RULES

It is very important to begin the finger exercises in the right way. They should be learned by heart, like all the music used in practice, so that full attention may be given to the hands. The following important rules may also be adopted.

1. Play all the finger exercises with a light touch at first, and above all play them evenly, with all the fingers giving equal power of tone. Practise each exercise for some days before trying to increase the force of the tone. To make the tones equal, there must be an unequal amount of pressure from the different fingers. The thumb is the strongest; then comes the third finger, then the fifth and second, and last of all is the weak fourth finger. The principle of treating the weakling with indulgence, so often met with in education, must not be followed here. The fourth finger must be made instead to give the greatest effort, to prevent inequality of tone. The ear is the guide, and the student must be able to hear when any undesired inequality begins to be evident. The tones will be equalized only after some practice.

2. Do not begin by repeating the finger exercises until tired. By practising with each hand singly, and changing hands often, the undesired fatigue may be avoided for quite a while. Gradually each hand may be kept at work for a longer time before changing; but even then one must avoid too much exertion. Let the hand rest as soon as it begins to feel heavy. If one does not stop or change at this point, the result will be a shakiness, or even a muscular pain, that will ultimately be very injurious.

3. Lower and raise the wrist at times while playing, in the same manner as directed in Section III while merely holding the notes. This procedure will prevent the hand from becoming stiff.

4. The fingers must not change their shape when raised from the keys, but must remain curved (see Figs. 4 to 8). The raised finger must not be bent inward or straightened out stiffly. These changes would not merely look bad, but would cause a decided waste of effort at the expense of speed and tone quality.

5. Notice the finger-tips carefully, and see that they strike the keys accurately; for that is the only way to obtain a full, strong tone.

6. It may be stated here that in playing a melody that is marked *forte,* or strongly accented, the black keys are to be struck with fingers outstretched rather than rounded. The fingers thus touch more of the key surface, and are less liable to slip off than if curved.

V. FINGER EXERCISES

1. FOR ONE FINGER

In the beginning it is best to take the simplest finger exercises, so that the attention may be devoted wholly to the position of the wrist and the action and position of the fingers.

While four fingers are used to press down the keys, as shown by the whole notes, one finger plays the quarter-notes.

Holding the hand as directed in Figs. 1 and 2, press down all five keys. Then raise the thumb just enough to let the key rise its full distance, keeping the thumb in contact with the key surface (see Fig. 4).

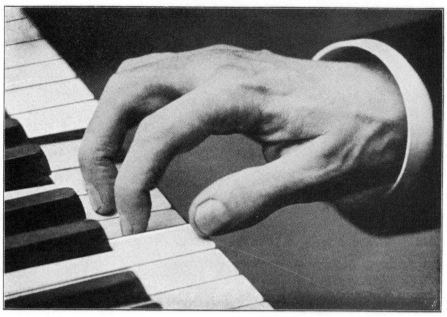

FIG. 4.

Let the thumb then press down the key till the tone is sounded. The tone should then be held with a further pressure, until the thumb is ready to end the tone by rising and keeping in contact with the key in preparation for the next tone. Repeat this exercise a number of times, and then go through the same

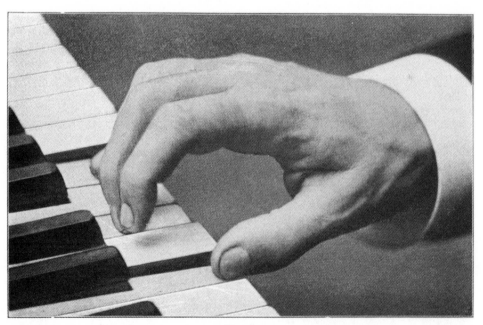

FIG. 5.

procedure with the second finger. Raise that finger until the key has risen, and a centimetre more, then press the key down and hold it with increased pressure as before. (See Fig. 5.)

Follow the same method with the third finger, keeping the others down. (See Fig. 6.)

Continue the exercise with the fourth and fifth fingers. (See Figs. 7 and 8.)

[EDITOR'S NOTE.—The holding of the fingers always in constant contact with the key surfaces, even with the keys raised, gives the *legato,* or "prepared," touch. By raising the fingers from the key, the *non-legato* style is obtained. The latter may be used along with the former. Mme. Brée gives the latter alone, but the prepared touch may receive most of the attention, as it is *harder* to acquire.]

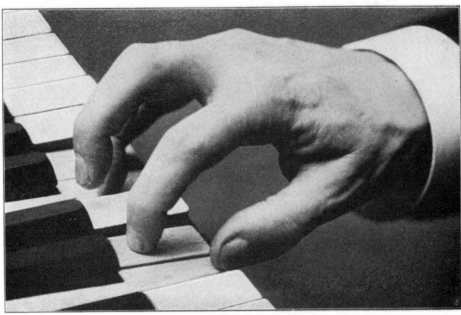

FIG. 6.

In practising these exercises with unprepared touch, the fourth and fifth fingers are to be raised as high as possible at first, so that the awkward fourth finger may acquire power of motion and the weak fifth may gain in strength. The wrist movement should be repeated during these exercises to prevent stiffness.

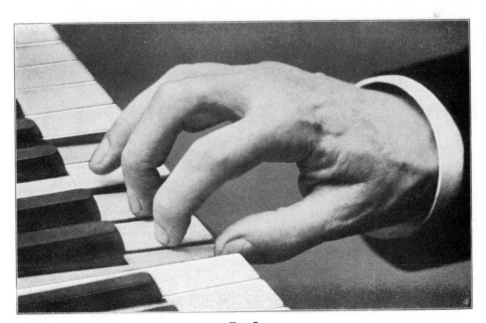

FIG. 7.

After going through these exercises *legato* for a time, practise them also *staccato.* (See Section XIV.) In this *staccato,* each finger strikes the key with a short, quick blow, and at once returns to its high position. This will increase the elasticity of the fingers.

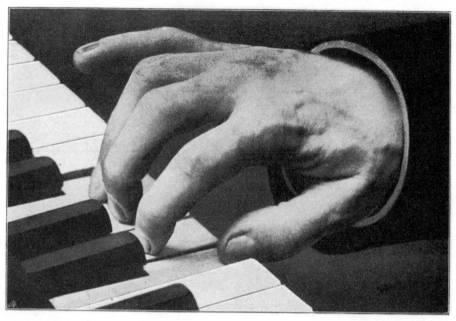

Fig. 8.

2. FOR TWO FINGERS

The two-finger exercises are based on the same principles, both with the prepared and the unprepared touch.

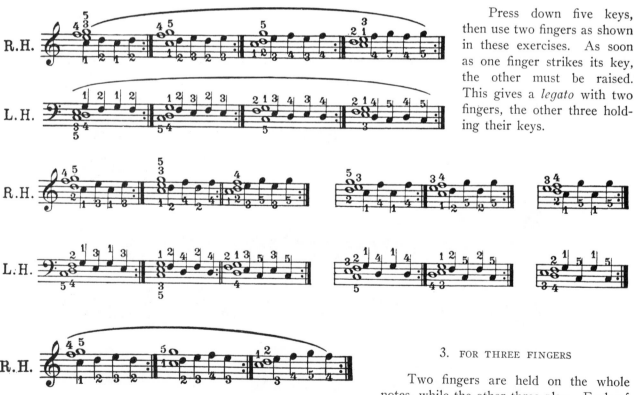

Press down five keys, then use two fingers as shown in these exercises. As soon as one finger strikes its key, the other must be raised. This gives a *legato* with two fingers, the other three holding their keys.

3. FOR THREE FINGERS

Two fingers are held on the whole notes, while the other three play. Each of the playing fingers is to hold its key down after striking, and is raised only just before its note is to be played.

4. FOR FOUR FINGERS

One note is held throughout, four are released and struck as above.

5. FOR FIVE FINGERS

Press down all five keys; then let each finger play in turn, while the other notes are held.

6. WITH ONE TONE HELD

Hold the whole note and play with the next finger, as printed. The other fingers are to be held high and kept rounded, excepting of course the thumb, which is to be bent loosely under the second finger (see Fig. 12, later on).

Do not let the action of the raised fingers become at all spasmodic, as that would detract from the strength of the active fingers. The fourth finger, however, may be expected to swing a little while the third is playing, and the fifth while the fourth is in use. This linking is caused by a certain tendon, and the resulting motion cannot be entirely avoided. In fact, the suppressing of this natural motion would cause actual harm, perhaps stiffening the wrist too much, as well as proving a long task.

7. WITHOUT HELD TONES

These exercises may be played *legato*, but without held tones. That is, as soon as any finger strikes a tone, the preceding finger may release its tone and be raised to its high rounded position. The thumb may be kept fairly close to its key.

There are hands with very movable finger joints, especially the middle joint of the thumb. Such a thumb may bend too far out from the knuckle joint, with the latter even showing an inward angle. This is apt to interfere with a strong tone or good octaves and chords. This undesirable and weakening action of the thumb knuckle can be overcome only by patience and attention. The following exercises, played softly with each hand alone, will prove useful.

The thumb must be held in its normal position, as in Fig. 1. If this proves hard, the thumb knuckle joint may be held out by the other hand, with the tip of its second finger; but too strong a pressure must be avoided.

Another unusual condition, the stiffness of the knuckle of the fifth finger, may be cured by the following exercise. Hold the note E pressed down by the third finger, with the other hand raise the fifth finger by its tip as high as possible, then play F repeatedly with the fourth finger as strongly as possible with a loose wrist. This method can be applied also to the naturally less flexible knuckle of the fourth finger. In this case the fourth is held up, while the fifth plays on G.

VI. Preparation for Diatonic Scales

When man was created, he was evidently not created a pianist; else he would have been provided with at least seven fingers on each hand, and each of the seven would have been of the same length as the others. Then he could have handled scales and chords, and been free from the necessity of "passing the thumb

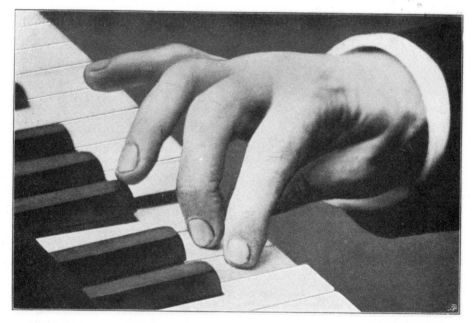

Fig. 9.

under" after three or four notes. But with our few and variable fingers, the turning-under requires a number of special exercises and steady practice.

With the thumb placed under the second and third fingers, and holding the note beyond the latter (above it in the right hand, below in the left), repeat each of the three notes a number of times, while the other two notes are held.

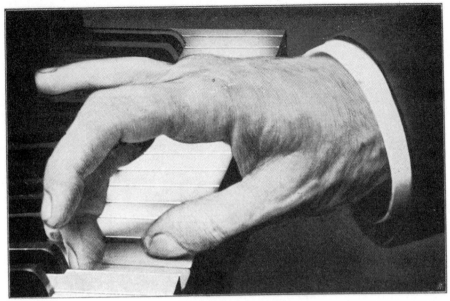

FIG. 10.

In these exercises one tone is held while two are played alternately.

In this exercise all three fingers play, each one holding its note after striking until it is necessary for the fingers to be raised in readiness to strike again. In these and the following exercises, it is advisable for the fingers that play just before or just after the thumb to give a little stronger tone than the others, in either upward or downward progression. This will minimize the unconscious tendency to start with emphasis when the thumb is turned under or the fingers swung over it. The notes requiring such emphasis are shown by dashes (*tenuto*).

The second and third fingers are allowed to hold their notes, while the thumb plays alternately in its normal place and in its bent-under position. The thumb must be kept bent a little, and never raised far from the keys in reaching up or down along its interval. The hand should be kept quiet during this exercise, with the wrist loose but quiet. The elbow should not rise when the thumb is passed under the fingers.

[EDITOR'S NOTE.—In all these exercises, it will be found that when the thumb is passed under the fingers, the latter are not to be kept straight forward as in the finger exercises. The right fingers bend about 45° toward the left hand, and *vice versa*. The hand will bend with them from the wrist, but the arm should not be moved away from the side. In complete scales extending to the extremities of the keyboard, the arm is very gradually moved away from the side, but the motion must be even and steady. As a result, the arm motion in the direction of the under-passing of the thumb accounts for a part of the interval that the thumb takes, and reduces the distance of each under-passing in actual scale playing. In the preparatory exercises, however, the arm moves very little from the side, and the thumb movement is aided by the change of the wrist toward a diagonal position during each under-passing. In scale-playing the hands may lean outward whenever necessary, with the little finger lowest.]

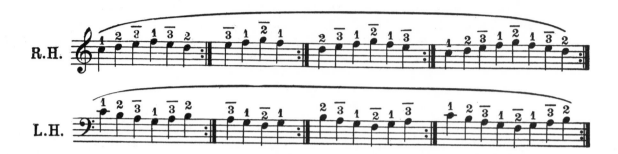

In these exercises, which have no held notes, but are merely played *legato,* the thumb is to be passed under the fingers as soon as it releases the note played in its normal position. The arm may move with each under-passing. (The forearm, however, moves along steadily, and does not follow any changing angles of the hand.)

VII. Similar Exercises, a Tone Wider

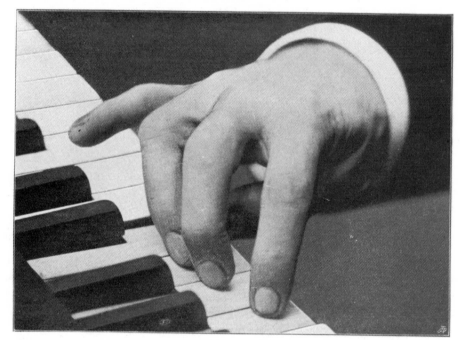

Fig. 11.

Each note is played repeatedly while the others are held.

Two notes are played alternately while the other two are held.

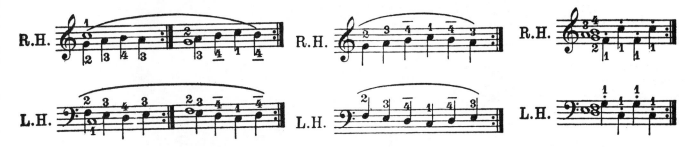

One note is held while three are played, and each of the three is to be held as long as possible after being played.

Four notes are played, each one being held as long as possible.

As before, notes are held by the fingers while the thumb plays alternately in its normal and under-passed position. The thumb, as before, must keep near the keys, while the wrist may turn more noticeably than when only two fingers were used with the thumb.

All notes to be played, with directions as for exercise with thumb and two other fingers.

[EDITOR'S NOTE.—These exercises, when the notes are not held down as long as possible, may be practised with the prepared touch even more often than with the unprepared touch. This preparation, or touching of key-surfaces while waiting for the proper time to play a note, will here be found somewhat difficult at first, but will prove of great value. In scale practice all tones are to be prepared as much as possible. Such an exercise as the following will prove useful: Play E with D and F prepared, the right thumb being under-passed for the F; then play the F with the thumb, shifting the fingers over as quickly as possible to prepare G, A, and B. Shift the hand back to prepare D and E, play E with the third finger while releasing the thumb to a prepared position, then play F and prepare the upper notes again, and so on. Another exercise consists of preparing and playing the notes D and E with second and third fingers (right hand), then quickly preparing and playing G, A, and B with second, third, and fourth fingers, then shifting again to D and E of the next higher octave, then upward to G, A, and B, and then reverse the process for the downward progression. Still another exercise, with the thumb included, runs thus: Play C with D and E prepared; play D and E together, preparing F with the thumb as quickly as possible; play F, preparing G, A, and B with the proper fingers as quickly as possible; play G, A, and B together, preparing C with the under-passed thumb as quickly as possible; play C, and continue as before through the octave above, ending with the little finger on the last note; then return through the two octaves, always preparing as quickly as possible the note or group below the one played. All these exercises must be taken in a reverse direction by the left hand. Any exercises suitable for the ascending scale may nearly always be reversed and practised by the same hand for the descending scale. The chromatic scale, *arpeggios,* and rapid exercises, will aid in improving scale-playing. Care must always be taken to let the second and fourth fingers play with as much power as the others, to make the scale even. Among the exercises are rapid triplets, chromatic intervals, and adjacent notes played with the thumb and fourth finger as well as the thumb and second. Rapid quadruplets, ascending and descending in series, are also valuable, while grace-notes also aid in gaining rapidity and evenness.]

VIII. Diatonic Scales

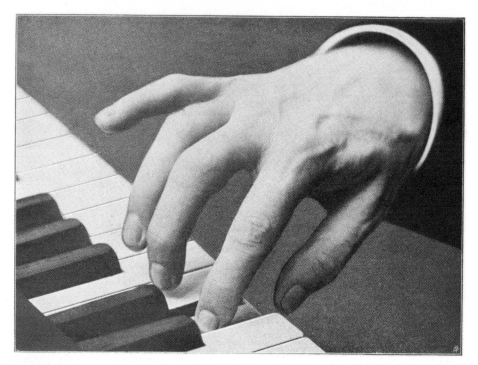

Fig. 12.

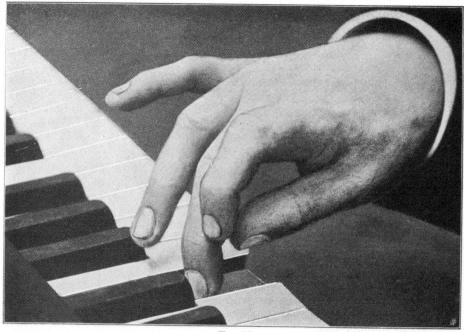

Fig. 13.

In scale playing the arm should not be made to jerk forward with the under-passing, but should move along smoothly like a train on the rails of its track. The wrist should be held loosely, but must not have any up-and-down motion. The fingers should be kept curved, though less so on the black keys than on the white.

Fig. 14.

As already mentioned, the thumb should pass under the fingers immediately after leaving its note, except when the upward scale ends in the right hand, and the downward in the left.

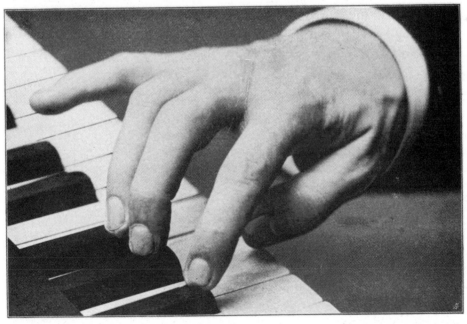

Fig. 15.

The scales should be practised very slowly at first, with a firm and even touch and no especial accents. Only after some time should the speed be gradually increased. One may count the notes in groups of three or four, but these groups must not be given any accent.

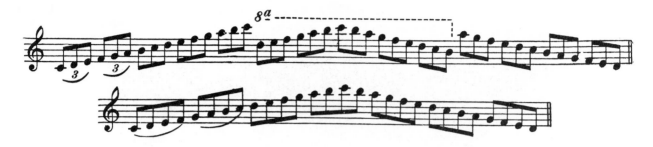

This is reversed for the left hand, starting down from middle C.

In rapid tempo the fingers are to be detached, or lifted quickly after each note almost as if for *staccato*. This will make the scale sound "pearly."

The scales may be practised at first by each hand alone, then with both together in contrary motion (giving the same fingering for both hands), and finally in parallel motion, both hands going up and down on the keyboard at the same time. This must be done in every key. When the student has mastered the slow scale with strong and even touch, he may practise it at different degrees of power—*forte, pianissimo,* and so on. Finally, he should play the scales *crescendo* and *diminuendo,* as the following will show, beginning again in slow *tempo.*

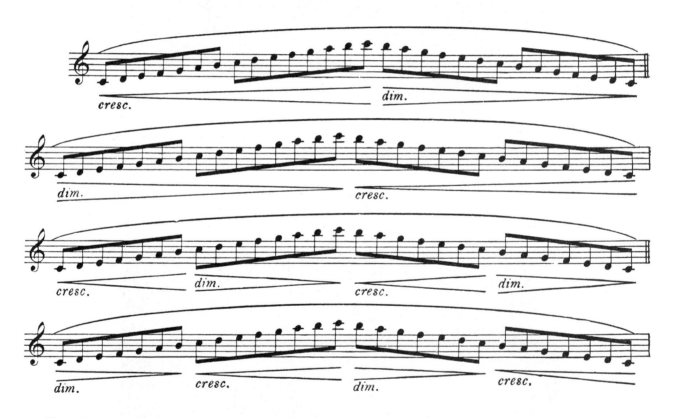

The left hand plays down two octaves. For directions regarding *crescendo* and *diminuendo,* see later section on Dynamics.

IX. THE CHROMATIC SCALE

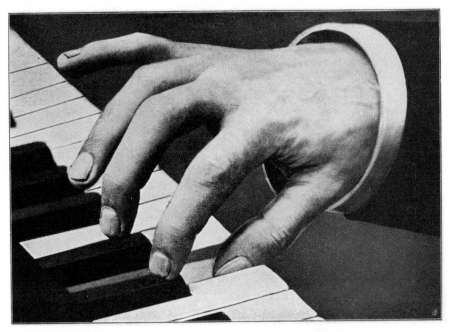

FIG. 16.

R.H.   L.H.

The thumb holds D a little nearer to the black keys than to the outer end of the white key. The second finger strikes C-sharp, then passes rapidly over to strike D-sharp, and repeats *ad lib*. As always, practise a similar exercise with the left hand.

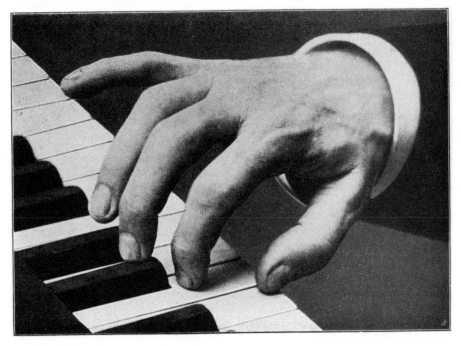

FIG. 17.

Without held notes. When the second finger comes on a white key, it may be bent as usual, but on the black keys it is somewhat less rounded. The wrist is held loosely, but should be a little higher for the

chromatic than for the diatonic scale. The thumb will thus strike the white keys more with the tip than the side. The fingers should strike the black keys near the front edge.

After the preparatory exercises have been duly mastered, the chromatic scale may be taken in groups of three or four notes, but without accents.

[EDITOR'S NOTE.—The tones of the chromatic scale are to be prepared as much as possible. Another good exercise may be made by running from D-sharp to G (left hand, G-flat to D), in which the thumb is prepared on G (left hand on D) after passing under the third finger. The exercises may be varied by practising any two adjacent keys together if the lower one is black (the upper one for the left hand), by playing one note while holding the other, playing one note with the other prepared, or alternating the two. The thumb will take the white key, and the second or third finger the black key, the third finger being used on F-sharp or C-sharp (left hand, B-flat or E-flat), while the second finger may come on any black key. In the actual scale the fingering may vary as shown, the third finger sometimes being passed over the thumb instead of the second, and the fourth finger being sometimes used at the upper end of the compass. The chromatic scale, like the diatonic, may be practised slowly, with varying power, with both hands in contrary motion, with both hands in parallel motion, and also in thirds, sixths, or tenths as well as octaves.]

X. PREPARATION FOR BROKEN TRIADS

The whole notes should be held throughout each exercise, with the hand well arched and the fingers curved. The wrist should be swung down and up a number of times, while the playing continues uninterruptedly.

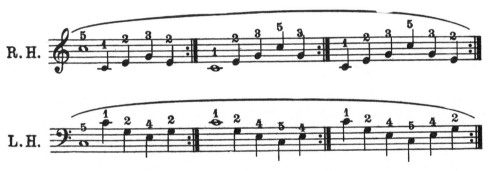

Directions as in preceding exercises, but let each finger hold its note after striking until it has to play again.

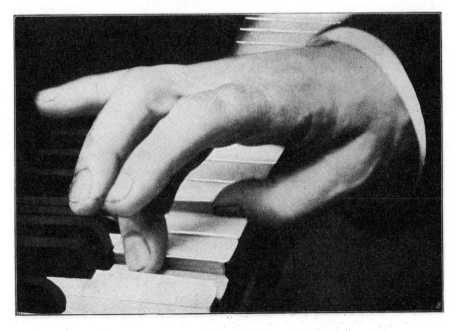

FIG. 18.

The whole notes are to be held throughout while the quarter-notes are played. Here, too, the **hand** **is** inclined inward from the wrist and the fingers arched for the under-passing of the thumb.

Without held notes. Except in the first bar, hand and arm move in the direction of the notes, the **latter** moving steadily and without jerks, while the former may swing sidewise from the wrist. Both thumb **and** fingers should move in a low curve, keeping near the keys.

Fig. 19.

Triad exercises in first and second inversion. Hand high and fingers well arched, as before.

These exercises are for players who can make a large stretch without unduly straining the hand. In the last exercise, the tones are to be held until necessarily released for repetition.

XI. BROKEN TRIADS

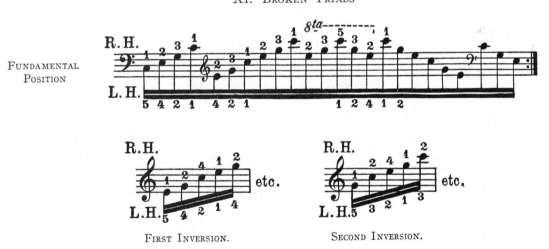

FUNDAMENTAL
POSITION

FIRST INVERSION.   SECOND INVERSION.

This exercise is to be practised first in the fundamental position and inversions of C major, and gradually extended to all other keys. The fingering given above applies to all keys, except when the second and third notes of a triad (first and second notes in the left hand) have one white and one black key. In that case (also with a small interval between the second and third fingers) the third finger may be used instead of the fourth. The third finger will be used for the first-position tonic triads with octave above the tonic when the left hand plays these in any sharp key except G. In the second inversion with octave above the dominant note, the right hand will need the third finger instead of the fourth in minor keys with more than one flat.

Another rule for fingering states that any broken triad beginning with a black key should be started by the second finger. It is also useful, however, to adopt as an exercise the principle of beginning any triad with the finger that would fall on its first note in the course of playing the broken triad up through more

than one octave. Thus the tonic triad of D-flat, even though begun with the second finger, would bring the fourth finger on the D-flat above, the thumb being passed under to F. So the triad may be practised beginning with the fourth finger instead of the second. In G minor the first inversion may be begun with the third finger, and so on.

XII. STUDIES FOR BROKEN SEVENTH CHORDS

These are to be played in all combinations and inversions, as for Section X.

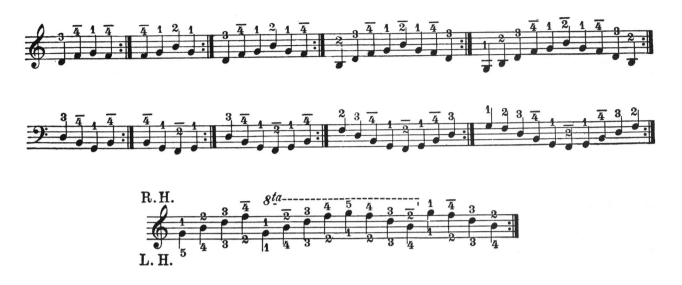

XIII. REPEATED NOTES WITH CHANGING FINGERS

When the same note is repeated with alternating fingers, they are to be moved from the knuckle joint, with hand and wrist quiet. The fingers should be held straighter than usual, and their tips slid toward the front end of the key. The wrist should be loose and rather high, so that the hand may turn slightly outward and aid the fingers in their motion. At first make only two fingers alternate, the outer one playing before its neighbor. Then carry the note, once repeated, through the diatonic scale, the broken triad, the dominant seventh chord, and the chromatic scale, as follows:

Then play a note three times, with the fingers 3, 2, and 1; also four times, with the fingering 4, 3, 2, 1. Use each hand alone. For repeating slow notes, better expression may be obtained by using the same finger without change.

XIV. Varieties of Touch

The piano student often assumes that finger exercises are "dry," and need no especial attention in performance. If so, however, he makes a great mistake, for the correctness of these exercises is every bit as important as the use of a proper method in practising singing. The excellence of touch and warm fulness of tone shown by the Leschetizky pupils is due to the fact that they have studied their finger-exercises in the correct way. The pianist should not forget the saying, *"C'est le ton qui fait la musique"*; and even if his tones cannot have the variety given by voice or violin, he should strive to master as many different styles of tone as possible.

In the first place, he must attain a well-developed *legato*. For this each finger must be kept on its key until the next finger strikes, and then lifted in the normal way. To obtain a *legatissimo*, the finger may continue to hold its note for a very small fraction of time *after* the next finger has struck.

When a strong, full tone is to be emphasized in a *cantilena,* the finger alone has not sufficient strength, and must be aided by wrist pressure in the following way. The key-surface is touched lightly and the finger then forced down by a movement of the wrist that brings the latter upward. Wrist and finger joints being held firm, the wrist tends to swing the hand down, but is moved up by the resistance of the key. The weight of the forearm is thus brought into play. The same result may be obtained by allowing the wrist to drop, in which case also as much weight may be employed as desired. Immediately after striking, the wrist must return to its normal position, and the finger hold the key down lightly. This will give a "singing tone," and should be practised with each finger.

[Editor's Note.—The *legato* is best practised with the prepared tone, keeping the finger in contact with the key-surface constantly. It is a good plan for the student to hold down all five notes with the fingers of one hand while preparing to play single notes. He may then count four for each tone, one being the releasing of a key, two the holding of the finger against the surface of the raised key, three the playing of the note (entirely by finger-power), and four a finger-pressure on the key after it is played. This exercise, which is very important, should be taken up at the beginning of piano study, and continued faithfully. It is indispensable for the control and development of the finger muscles, and should be played without the slightest pressure of the arm. It will be found advisable to use the device of skipping a white key between the second and third fingers, so that the motion will be always as nearly vertical as possible. The fourth finger must not be strained at first, but must increase its power of tone gradually. When the fingers are lifted from the keys, as Mme. Brée directs, the result is used in what Leschetizky would now call a *non-legato*. In this the student may count eight—two for the releasing of the key, two more for the raising of the finger from the key-surface, one for the falling of the finger to the key-surface, one for the pressing down of the key (playing the note), and two for the after-pressure. The fourth finger, which cannot at first raise itself any distance, may be lifted by the other hand until it can rise sufficiently by itself. Both of these important exercises may be practised also on five adjacent keys. The notes may be given with varying speed and power. Similar exercises for two, three, and four fingers should be practised, with each note held as long as possible before being played again. All these may be given *crescendo* and *decrescendo,* as well as wholly soft or loud.]

For *staccato,* the fingers are not pressed, but struck from above and released immediately. For the finger-*staccato,* as for the *non-legato,* the fingers may be raised fairly high, and in this case the wrist may be bent back a little, with the thumb kept on or near its key-surface. Power is furnished from the knuckles. Each finger must strike its key rapidly, and rise at once after the stroke. In rapid *tempo* the staccato approaches the *non-legato,* because each finger strikes quickly after the preceding one. The finger-staccato may be practised at first on five tones, and afterward through all the scales. Begin slowly, increasing the speed later. The thumb may be bent under the palm when not used, much as in the *legato* scales.

In the wrist *staccato* the bent fingers strike upon the keys rapidly, and are drawn up at once by the throwing-back of the wrist.

The "lifted tone," or soft wrist *staccato,* is obtained by having the fingers touch the key-surfaces, while after a note or chord is played from this position the fingers are all drawn up quickly by the throwing back of the wrist. The "lifted tone" may be practised at first on single notes, then on five notes and on chords. In the following example, the notes marked with an asterisk are played with "lifted tone."

In the following, the starred note goes best as a "lifted tone" with pedal.

In the stronger wrist-*staccato,* the fingers are lifted with the wrist, and a blow struck from above the keys by the swinging of the wrist downward. The wrist should immediately be brought back to its raised position, as if rebounding from the keyboard. The motion should be wholly free from any sidewise direction, and the fingers held in the position needed for the notes before the wrist begins to descend.

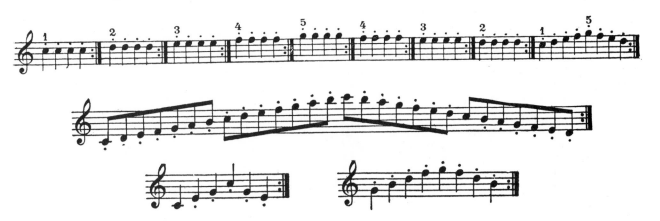

In the upper line, hand and fingers must keep their position over the proper keys, without moving sidewise.

The scales and broken chords may be played in all keys. The latter may be taken through one octave at first, in each inversion, and then through two and three octaves. The sidewise motion of the fingers may be followed yieldingly with the wrist, but each stroke should be as nearly vertical as possible. Some sound will come from the rapping of the finger-tips on the notes, but this does no harm if not exaggerated, and may even suit a burlesque effect, as in Mendelssohn's Scherzo, op. 16.

In this style of *staccato,* the wrist motion must of necessity be shortened in rapid passages. In very rapid work the fingers have to remain close to the keys, and flutter up and down a short distance.   This will be the case in the *prestissimo* passage, from Beethoven's Sonata, op. 10, No. 1.

The *portamento,* consisting of tied notes with dots over them, is not to be played *staccato.*   Each note is pressed down firmly with a prepared touch, held firmly for most of its value with a dropped wrist, and released by a lifting of the forearm.

XV. OCTAVES

The following is practised with each hand, as a preparatory study.   The whole note may be held by the tip of the little finger or the side of the thumb near its tip, while the other note is played by a rotating

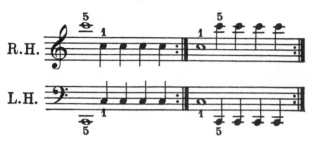

of the wrist sidewise, and a firm finger or thumb.   This exercise will be found strengthening, but must not be kept up long enough to produce fatigue.   Large hands may use the fourth finger on black keys instead of the fifth.   For part of the time the exercise may be varied by raising the thumb or finger until the hand is perpendicular to the keys, and then dropping the hand back to play the note.

It is also possible to impress the feeling of an octave on the hand by merely preparing the thumb and fifth (or fourth) finger on the outer edges of their notes.   The rest of the hand is of course held high.

After this the actual octaves may be taken up, with the use of the rebounding wrist-*staccato* when only moderate power is needed.   The distance between the thumb and fifth finger must be kept unchanged, so that all octaves may be struck squarely.

The above exercises are to be played slowly and strongly at first, with increasing speed later on.   The hand will be forced to remain nearer the keys as the speed increases, and will flutter up and down.

Broken chords in octaves are hard to play on the white keys when the size of the intervals changes. The student may obviate this difficulty by naming the notes or intervals mentally as he strikes them, in which case the fingers will soon grow accustomed to the proper interval after each note.

When *forte* or *fortissimo* octaves are needed, they must be played with a firm and high-held wrist, the fingers never moving far above the keys, and a stiff forearm aiding to produce the power.

For *legato* octaves also the fingers must be kept close to the keys.   The wrist is practically quiet, but not stiff.   In moving outward from the middle of the keyboard, the thumbs may be held as if playing *glissando.*   It is often advisable to use the fifth finger on white keys, and the fourth finger on black.   When the keys used are all white or all black, the fifth and fourth fingers may be used as below in *legato* work.

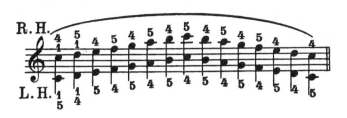

Hands with small reach or little strength may use the fifth finger.

When the octaves go fluently, they may be practised uninterruptedly on a tone or a scale, until fatigue sets in.

Leschetizky, while young, employed alternating octaves in place of simple ones, as in the following. The device is much used now.

The second passage replaces the first, the thumb notes being given the most force in each hand.

[EDITOR'S NOTE.—All the finger exercises given in previous sections may be practised in octaves, both soft and loud. Kullak's "Octave School" is always a valuable reference in this connection.]

XVI. CHORDS

Chords are to be pressed rather than struck. When a chord is struck from any height, its tones sound hard, and do not carry well. A chord may be pressed down in the following way. Arch the hand as far as the needed interval will permit; curve the fingers; and keep the finger-tips and wrist firm. The stroke is to be like that described in Section XIV, for *legato* in a *cantilena,* and is performed by letting the wrist swing up as the fingers go down, as if the knuckles were a fulcrum until the notes were struck, or else by letting the wrist drop with the weight of the forearm. In a series of slow chords, either motion may be used, but in rapid chord-passages, the upward swing of the wrist is best. To obtain more power, make the movement more extensive.

To avoid excessive fatigue from chord-playing, it is necessary to relax the stiff wrist after the chords have been struck, and to hold them with only enough power to keep the notes down. The hand may also assume any comfortable position between chords.

To make sure of striking a chord correctly, it may be prepared separately. The fingers may be put on the key-surfaces until their relative position and stretch is fully noted. The chord, however, is not to

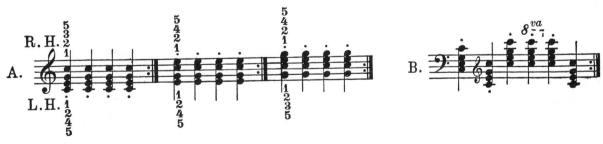

be played from the prepared position, but from a more or less raised position, according to the amount of force desired, or the speed. After some practice the hand will be able to adjust itself for any chord without the preliminary preparation. This will prove of especial value for the chord-skips that are often found in modern display-pieces.

Each of these exercises should be practised with both kinds of attack, taking the upward wrist first and making the chords very short in this case. The upward wrist and brief holding of chords is shown in the first following example, from Rachmaninoff's well-known Prelude.

In a piece which contains a slow succession of chords, the upward movement may be given more scope, so that not only the hand, but the arm also, is raised. This is especially advisable when *forte* or *fortissimo* chords are to be cut off sharply, as in the example above.

The first chord-exercises given here may also be practised with a rebounding stroke, as for wrist *staccato*. They are not to be played this way, as the tone will not be so good, but the exercise will prove beneficial. There are, in fact, many cases in which chords have to be struck, as there is no time in some rapid passages for the preparation needed for the other methods. An example is found in Liszt's Tenth Rhapsody.

In connection with the first chord-exercises given here, the following points may be noted. If a chord is repeated, as in exercise A, the raised hand must retain the shape needed for playing it. If there are skips from one chord to another, as in exercise B, the first chord is pressed down and abandoned quickly, the hand being carried over to the next chord in a rapid swing. When successive chords differ in their intervals, the hand must take the shape needed for the coming chord while still in the air.

Still another bit of advice will help the student to avoid needless fatigue. When chords succeed one another slowly, with rests between them, the uplifted hand may be bent each time into the shape of a fist. This radical change of position will give the hand a period of rest each time it is used. Rubinstein employed this procedure, and Leschetizky does the same.

The fingering for chords, and the exceptions, are the same as the fingering and exceptions for broken chords given in Section XI.

In the following pages are found pictures illustrating the various positions of the hand for all the chords beginning on C. They will give the proper shape of the hand, as well as the fingering. The chords may be practised with the preliminary preparation suggested above, though they should be played from a raised position. The chords may be played on one beat first, then as broken chords in a single octave, and finally as arpeggios extending through two or more octaves. After practising the chords on C, the student may take those on D-flat, and so on in succession through the entire chromatic range. This study will have a theoretical as well as a technical value.

Fig. 20.

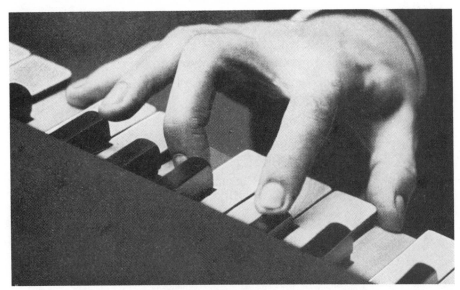

Fig. 21.

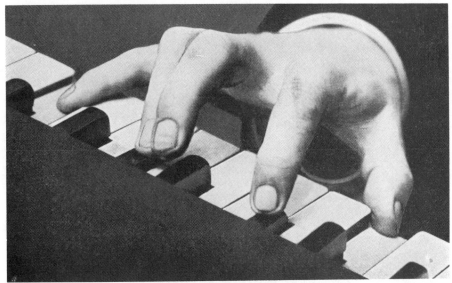

Fig. 22.

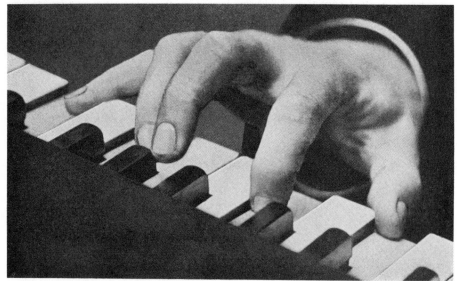

Fig. 23.

Fig. 24.

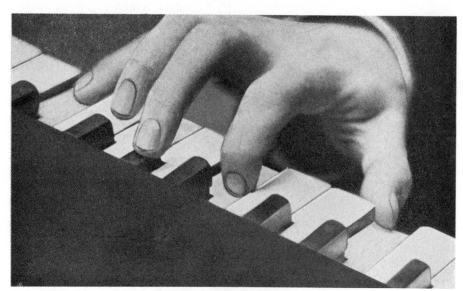

Fig. 25.

FIG. 26.

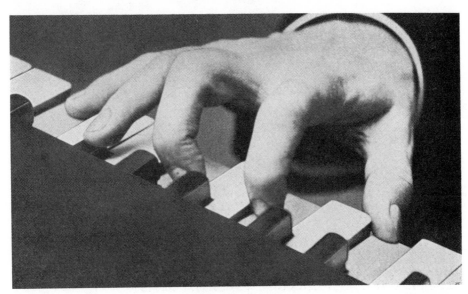

FIG. 27.

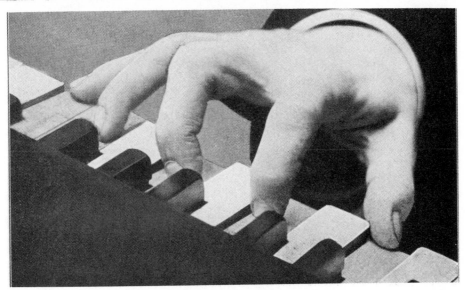

FIG. 28

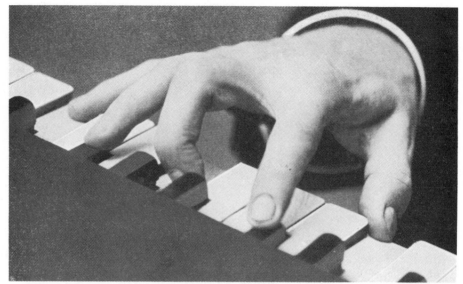

Fig. 29.

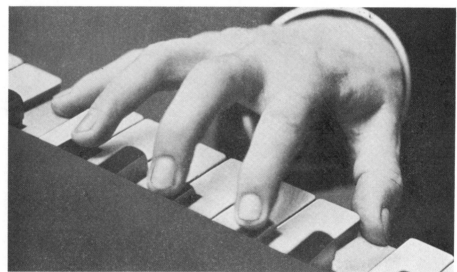

Fig. 30.

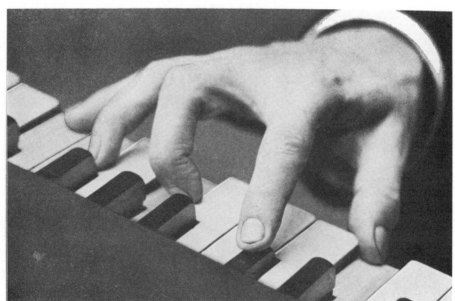

Fig. 31.

Fig. 32.

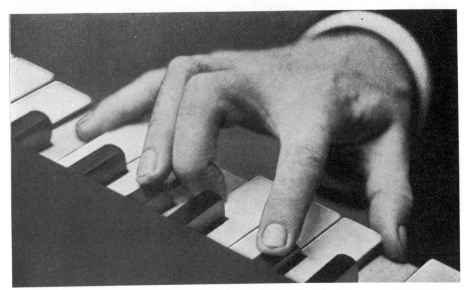

Fig. 33.

Fig. 34.

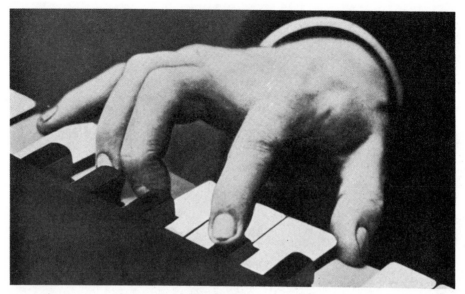

FIG. 35.

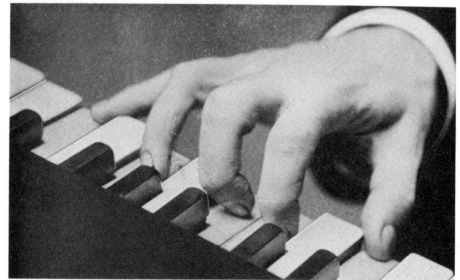

FIG. 36.

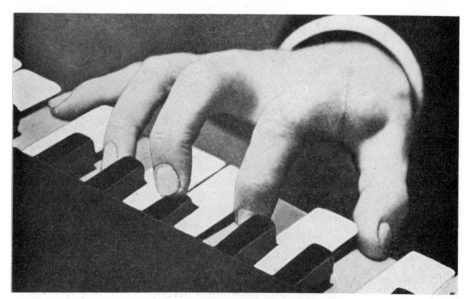

FIG. 37.

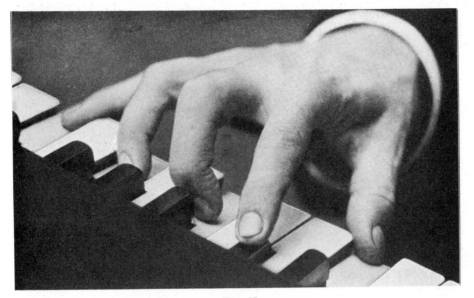

FIG. 38.

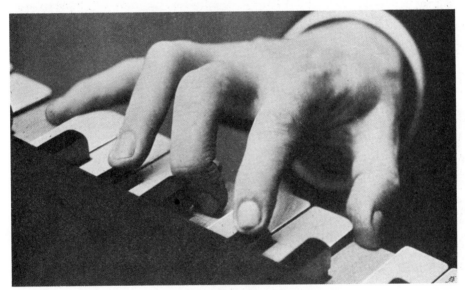

FIG. 39.

FIG. 40.

FIG. 41.

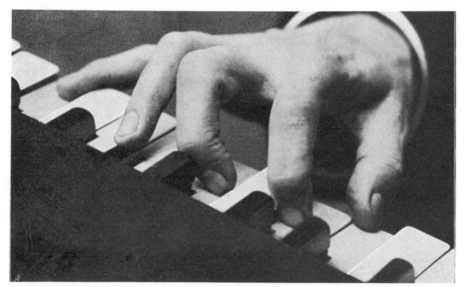

FIG. 42.

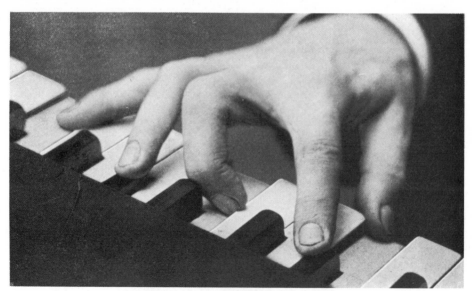

FIG. 43.

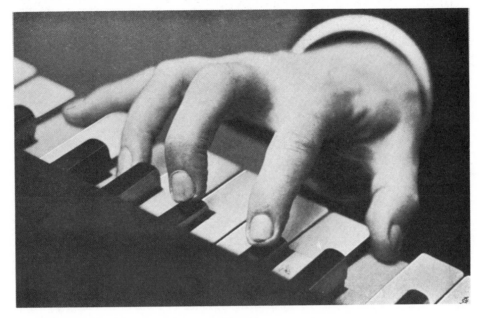

FIG. 44.

XVII. ARPEGGIOS

In the first instance, the first three fingers are held ready over their keys, with the fifth finger extended somewhat to the right. The first three fingers play their notes in succession, and the hand is then given a quick inclination to the right, letting the fifth finger strike its key. The wrist motion for this is a slight rotation, not unlike that used in turning a key in a lock. The fifth finger may shorten its note, as that gives the note prominence. The hand may then return quickly to its normal position, in readiness for the next *arpeggio.*

For *arpeggios* with both hands, do not begin at the same time in both hands, but let the left hand finish and the right hand then continue the *arpeggio,* the right thumb following just after the left.

 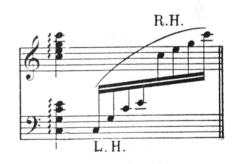

[EDITOR'S NOTE.—It is usual in modern music-printing to mark the *arpeggio* by one continuous line across both staffs, when the *arpeggio* is to be played as directed above. The two separate marks are now taken to mean that each hand has its own *arpeggio,* and that the two do begin together. The preparatory exercises for extended *arpeggios,* which are practically rapid broken chords in many cases, involve the under-passing of the thumb, the over-passing of the fingers if the *arpeggio* proceeds toward the centre of the keyboard, and a gradual, steady motion of the arm away from the side or toward it. A preliminary exercise may consist of holding G with the third finger of the right hand and under-passing the thumb to play the C above. The left hand may hold F with the third finger and under-pass to the C below. The right hand may hold A with the fourth finger, and under-pass to C, while the left hand may go through a similar process by holding E with the fourth finger and under-passing to the C below. These may be varied by letting the thumb hold its note while the fingers play. Thumb and finger may then play alternately. The thumb, being bent, will have to strike the key near its outer end, while the finger must be well rounded. The force may be varied from p to f. A second variety of exercise consists of connecting the various parts of an *arpeggio*. The right hand may play G with the third finger, while holding the C above it prepared with the thumb. The C is then to be played, the second and third fingers meanwhile being prepared as quickly as possible on the E and G above it. The left hand may practise an exercise symmetrical with this. Both hands may then be taken through the broken-chord *arpeggio* for two octaves, preparing each tone as soon as it becomes possible. Other chords may then be employed, and the *arpeggio* in each case reversed in direction.]

XVIII. Paired Notes

For these exercises the hand is to be held as in the finger exercises of Section V, with the wrist loose. The whole notes are held while the quarter-notes are played.

In the first two of these exercises, the whole notes are to be held, the others played. In the next two exercises, the first third is to be held as long as possible, the thumb holding its note until the repeat.

The next exercise is to be played without any held tones (see Figs. 45 and 46).

The line below illustrates over-passing (or rather side-passing) in thirds. In example A press down the keys with the second and fourth fingers, in example B with the third and fifth. Then take the next third, with first and third fingers, by swinging sidewise with a high wrist. Then swing the wrist back for the recurrence of the first third, and continue as before. In going up with the right hand, the fourth or fifth finger may be used as a point of support, and the thumb in coming down. The reverse, of course, is true of the left hand.

As it is impossible to play all the notes *legato*, it is merely necessary to hold as long as possible the tone played by the finger that acts as the point of support. The other finger may be lifted from its key as soon as the swinging movement is started.

FIG. 45.

[EDITOR'S NOTE.—In playing double notes, care must be taken to strike them both together, and to emphasize the upper note more than the lower one. For the latter effect, great care must be taken to see that the weak fourth finger gives its notes with due strength. It is even advisable to practise letting this finger take its note alone, the companion note being touched but not played. When both notes are played throughout, the fourth finger may be allowed to give a noticeable accent for practice. In playing a scale of thirds, it will

FIG. 46.

be found useful to let the right hand turn outward a little while ascending, and the left while descending. Both hands may be turned inward a little when returning toward the centre of the keyboard. In playing the scale of C (see below) with the right hand, the first three thirds come in normal position. The second third may be prepared while the first is sounding. When the second pair of notes is struck, the thumb is bent under the hand and the third and fifth fingers prepared. When the latter have struck, the fifth finger is used for support, the third finger being lifted and passed over it to A (moving close to the keys), while the thumb is prepared on F. When F and A are played, the second and fourth fingers are prepared on G and B. As the latter strike, the third finger is passed over and prepared on C, while the thumb is prepared on A, near which it falls naturally. In descending, great care must be taken when the other fingers are passed beyond the first and third. If the fourth finger passes by the third to a black key the hand may be turned quite noticeably. But if the fourth passes to a white key while the third holds a black key, the fourth finger may be readily prepared under the third. In general, a *legato* effect is suggested if the upper notes are fairly well linked; but when this is not possible, the linking may be made by the finger used for support. Similar care in over-passing and under-passing is needed for scales or runs in sixths. But it is worth while to practise the thirds and sixths without preparation for part of the time, or even *staccato*.]

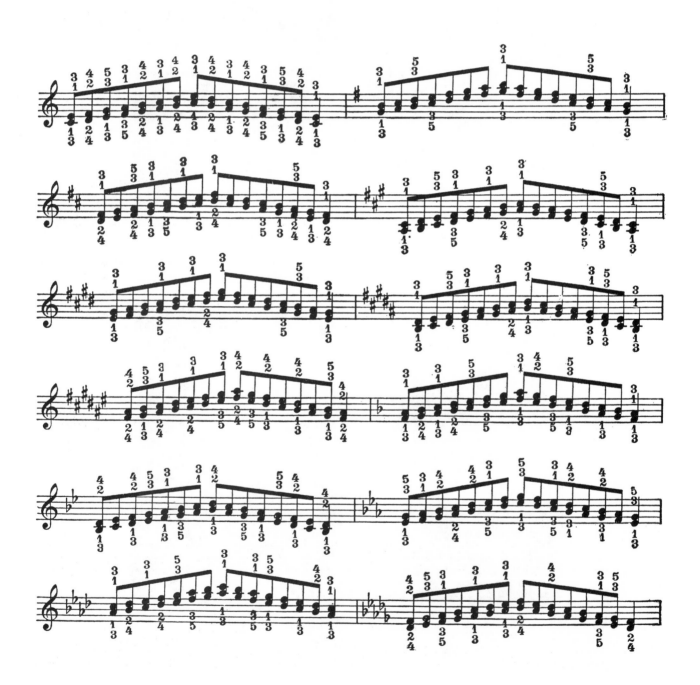

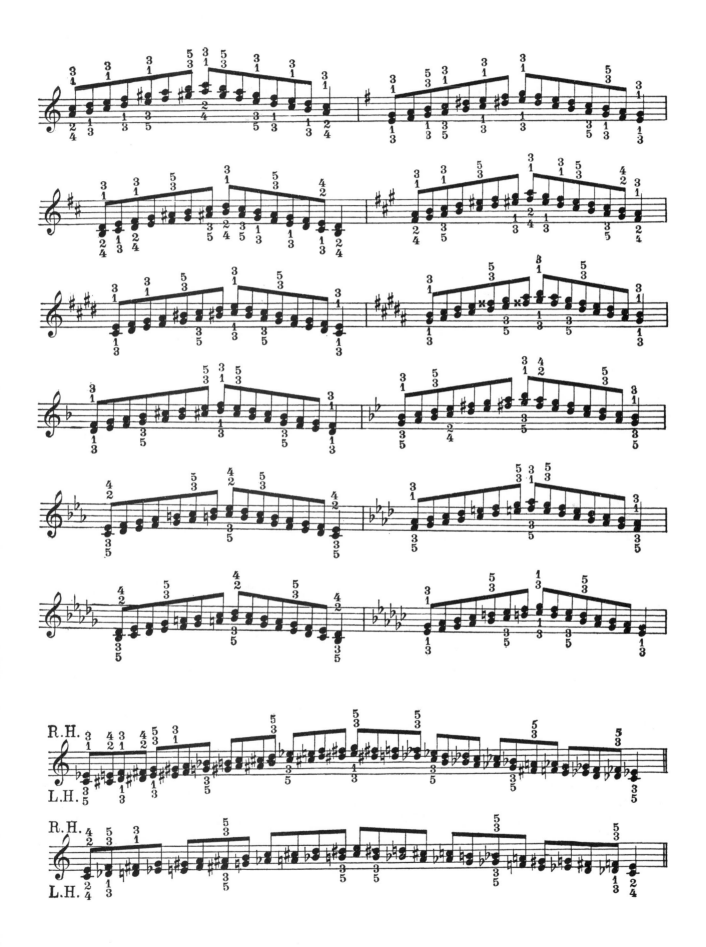

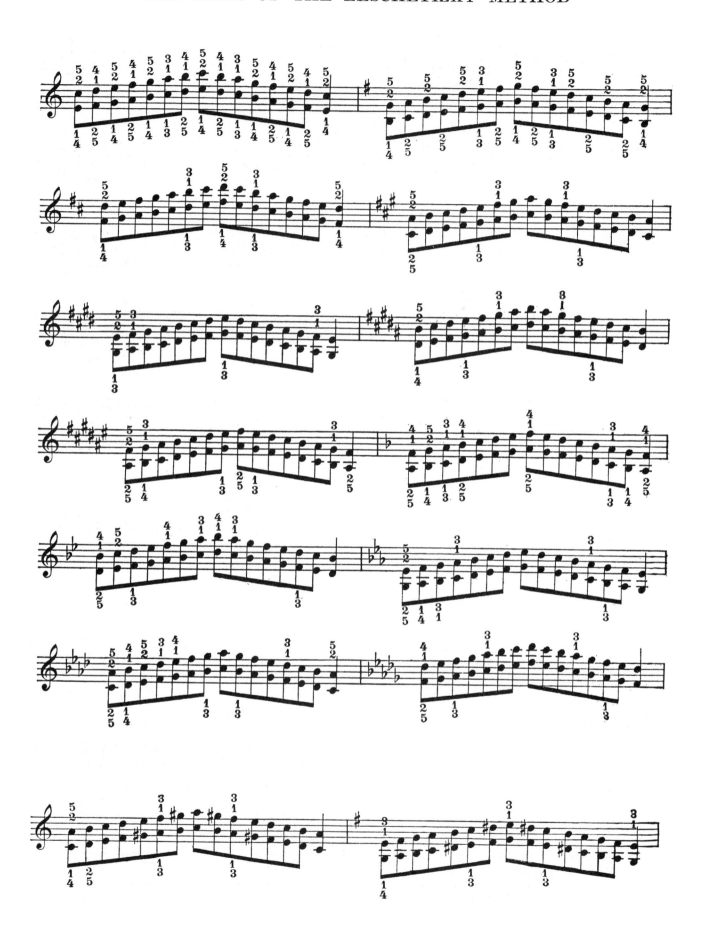

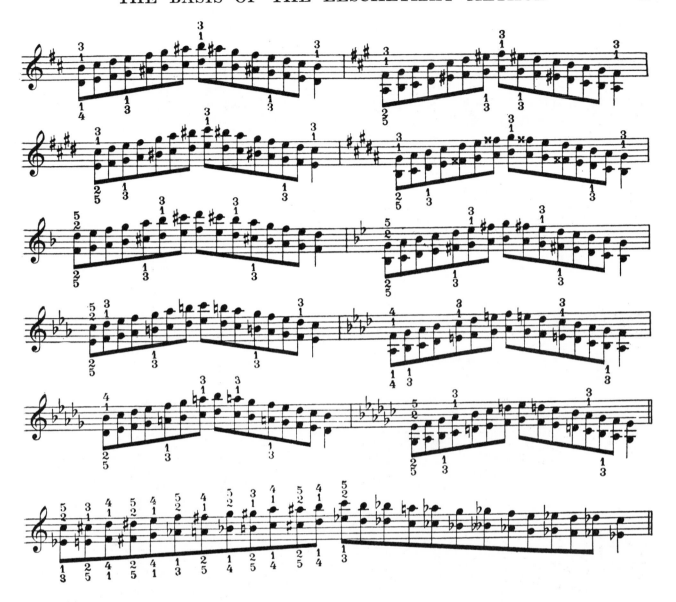

XIX. The Upper Part in Chord Playing

In chords, there is often a melodic idea that lies in the highest part. To bring this melody out (when the chords are not played *arpeggio*) it is practicable to elongate the finger that plays the part, while keeping the other fingers more rounded. The stretched-out finger will touch the white keys below its tip, and will be flat on the black keys. As a result, this finger will press its note down deeper and more powerfully than the others, thereby obtaining the fullest tone. The wrist is to be held high and firm in playing the chord, and should put more pressure on the melody-finger

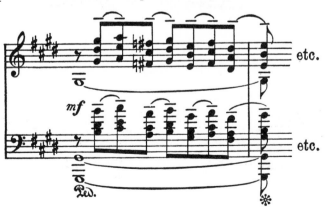

than on the others. After the chord is played, the wrist may relax and take its normal position, to rest for the next chord. If it is possible to take the pedal with the chord, it then becomes practicable to release the lower notes quickly and hold the melody notes by putting down the pedal after the others are released.

In the foregoing illustration from Rachmaninoff's Prelude, the highest part may be linked as much as possible, while the lower notes of each chord are released, after being struck, by a lift of the wrist.

p dolce

The fifth finger is generally the one to give the melodic idea. Sometimes, however, some other finger does this work, or the melody-notes may lie in the middle of the chords; but the same directions apply as before. The above, from Brahms, op. 117, is an example.

XX. The Glissando

When perfectly done, the *glissando* becomes an ideal diatonic scale, for it sounds very "pearly" when given rapidly and evenly. This is a case where these false pearls are more dazzling than the genuine ones, the former being more perfect and more like one another. That is to say, a *glissando,* when smoothly and evenly done, sounds better than the ordinary scale. But the *glissando* must show no jerks or uneven spurts, and the finger-nail must not scratch the keys audibly in its passage. To end with due emphasis on the proper note, the finger may be allowed to slide down over the front edge of the key in question, which will give a suitable accent.

The third finger may be employed for both upward and downward directions (Fig. 47). It is easier and more customary to let the right thumb take the downward *glissando,* and any one who can achieve good

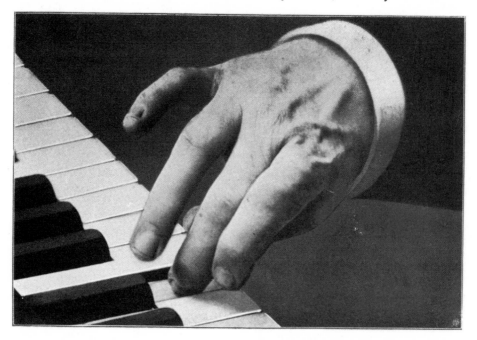

Fig. 47.

results by this means is at liberty to use his own method; but generally the third finger will give a smoother tone.

The *glissando* may be given with any desired power, in accordance with the pressure exerted on the keys.

The octave *glissando* is possible only for large and strong hands. The little finger is bent outward to take the upper notes with its nail, while the thumb plays the lower notes with the nail-edge farthest from the fingers. The fingers slope in the opposite direction for a downward *glissando.*

XXI. Embellishments

To make embellishments really worthy of their name, they must be executed clearly and elegantly, but also with crispness and sharp outline. Most important are the grace-notes, the mordent, the turn, and the trill. Regarding the short grace-note (*acciaccatura*), it will be sufficient to note that it is played on the beat, and not before it, being given with the notes in the other hand, and followed as quickly as possible by the note to which it is prefixed. In the case of an *arpeggio* chord with a short grace-note, the latter may become part of the *arpeggio*, taking its place in an upward series that begins coincidently with the left-hand notes. In this case some of the notes may be held by the pedal.

The mordent usually has the accent come on the principal note. It is best played with the third and fourth fingers of the right hand, so that the strong third finger can give the accent, either on the principal note or on the first note. When weaker fingers have to play a mordent, a special effort is needed for equalization of tone and proper accent.

In rapid *tempo* the mordent may be played as a triplet. The example opposite is from Leschetizky's Arabeske, op. 45, the triplets being merely mordents written out.

For the turn over a note, the following fingering is best, although sometimes the melodic structure enforces the fingering 3-2-1-2. The turn after a note is also best played with the second, third, and fourth fingers.

The trill is by far the most important of the embellishments. In the first place, even pressure of the fingers is necessary; for a slow trill given evenly sounds much better than a rapid trill that is uneven. The best trill, of course, is both even and rapid. The difference of strength in the different fingers must be neutralized by varying their pressure. For the right hand, 1 and 3 give the best results. Three and 5, or even 2 and 4, are sometimes used. Two and 3 are widely favored, but their value is often over-estimated. One and 2 are of course strong. For the left hand, 1 and 2 are best, with 2 and 3 a close second. The other notes of a piece will often determine which fingers are to be used, as in Beethoven's Sonata, op. 111.

It is advisable to practise the trill in triplets, going slowly at first and accenting the first note of each triplet. Later on the speed may be increased, and the accent dropped. This should be done with each pair of adjacent fingers, as marked.

A trick suitable for a loud trill consists of beginning by striking both notes nearly together, sforzando; the finger on the principal note is then raised, the note struck by another finger, and the trill continued.

[EDITOR'S NOTE.—Another trick in this connection is Liszt's so-called vanishing trill, on a semitone near the middle of the keyboard, with pedal. After the trill has grown constantly softer, the two notes are finally held together, the upper note being played again very lightly every second or so afterward. The beats between the notes give the effect of an extremely light and ethereal prolonging of the trill.]

Trills may be played by each pair of fingers for endurance. The strongest fingers can hardly hold out a minute, but the exercise is very beneficial.

In long trills, a change from one fingering to another is useful in preventing needless fatigue. Two and 3 may be succeeded by 1 and 3, etc.

The fingering for trills in thirds is shown here. If it is more convenient to use the third finger instead of the fourth, it may be done.

[EDITOR'S NOTE.—Some of the two-finger exercises in section V may be taken as a start in practising for the trill. They may be taken at varying degrees of speed and power, with the other fingers either pressing down their keys, or completely off them, or resting prepared upon the key surfaces. In a *decrescendo* trill, it is practicable to start with the strongest fingers, and shift afterward to weaker ones. When the left hand is free to aid the right, a number of effects may be obtained. In a chain of trills, in which the principal note must always have a full share of emphasis, that note may be struck loudly at first by the left thumb. If the lower note is played wholly by a left-hand finger, and the upper note wholly by a right-hand finger, the force-trill results. This trill, introduced by Henri Ketten, can be made tremendously powerful, though it is usual to shade the force-trill off at its end by the use of one hand alone. All trills should be played *legato*. One-hand trills should be given by finger-strength alone. The subject of trills is well treated in vol. 4 of J. A. Pacher's *"Der Pianist der guten Schule."*]

XXII. DYNAMICS

The subject of dynamics, or the science of force, deals with the use and variation of the different degrees of power in playing.

There are but three main things to note—loudness, softness, and accent. Of these alone is the scheme of tonal power constructed, by frequent and skilful alterations or transitions.

Forte and *fortissimo* cannot be performed by the fingers alone, but demand also the strength of wrist and arm. The finger-tips must be held firmly, and the wrist tense. The true *fortissimo* is the result of both finger and wrist or arm power, often increased by the use of the pedal.

Where the succession of tones is slow, equal strength is used for each note, whether in *piano* or *forte*. In the former, however, the keys being pressed lightly, there is time to push them down slowly with the prescribed after-pressure, which produces the soft, singing tone. In soft passages the wrist is kept loose; but the finger-tips must be held firm, or the tone-quality may seem dull. In rapid passages the fingers are swung down, with the wrist still loose. Faint *pianissimo* passages on the black keys may be given a light, fluttering character by being played with the fingers stretched out flat and held firmly, as in the following example from Chopin's Berceuse.

Accent is a decisive prominence given to individual tones by strong or sudden pressure, for melodic, harmonic, or rhythmic reasons. Accents, from the slightest to the strongest, are to be obtained with firm fingers and a firm wrist. When the accented note is to be held for some time, the wrist may relax and the finger merely hold the note after it is struck; or the tone may be sustained entirely by pedal if the latter is called for. For a short accented note, the pedal is not used, the hand being quickly withdrawn after the desired length of tone.

In a *crescendo,* the wrist may be loose at first and become stiff gradually. For a *diminuendo* the reverse is true, the stiff wrist gradually relaxing. The change in either case must be made evenly, and not by any sudden alteration. If necessary, the student may let his imagination assist his hands, and picture to himself the increasing noise of an approaching train, or the gradual quieting of a receding one.

In passages of rapid notes, the tone to be most strongly marked is the dynamic climax of a *crescendo,* which usually coincides with a beat, as indicated by the asterisk in the following example.

In playing a *crescendo* or *diminuendo,* care must be taken not to exceed the range of power demanded. The requisite change must be made without letting the *crescendo* grow too loud, or the *diminuendo* too soft, for the passage that follows it.

XXIII. THE PEDAL

For many good people (but bad performers) the pedal is a device for trampling on good taste and crushing it under foot. Aside from the fearful and wonderful effects produced by the *dilettanti,* there are two classes of professional musicians who use the pedal more or less wrongly. First, there are those who follow directions with a pedantic accuracy, but seem horrified at the slightest variation from strict harmonic law. These do no harm, but succeed in avoiding nearly all the interesting effects. Secondly, there are the pianists who rely on a good ear and a correct instinct, without considering the pedal as an important subject for study. These players will sometimes give artistic results, but their effects vary too much in different performances. The pedal is quite as important as any other department of piano practice, and demands fully as much care and attention. Its main purpose is to reinforce the tone and to link separate notes together; but it can also produce many special effects. These are to be sought for by the performer, for it would cause too much trouble for the composer if he had to put all the details of pedaling into his manuscript.

In the main, the ear is the correct guide, and Euphony plays a more important rôle here than Theory. But the performer should first study out what pedaling he desires. Then, if the ear approves of his decision, he should make this pedaling a part of his practice. Dissonances are more noticeable at a distance than near by, but the performer can judge them well also if he prolongs the pedaling.

The pedal (of course the damper pedal is meant) may be pressed down either with the playing of a note, or after the note is struck. The latter is called a "syncopated," or "following," pedal.

The simultaneous pedal is used to hold a note that should sound after the finger is forced to release the note. In the following instance, the lowest note must sound through the whole bar, although the finger leaves it.

The syncopated pedal can be employed where the tone to be sustained is held for a sufficient time before the next note or notes are struck. In the illustration, small notes are printed to show when the pedal is to be depressed.

The syncopated pedal may be practised in this way, striking the note to be held and then putting the pedal down just before releasing the note. The chord in the exercise is then played, and the pedal held right through until the next single note is struck.

Mendelssohn's Song Without Words, No. 1, with its frequent changes of harmony, is a good study for syncopated pedal effects.

Here the first two sixteenths with each quarter-note are mostly easy to hold, so that the pedal may usually come on the second half of each beat. If the pedal were taken throughout each beat, the effect would not be so light and dainty. The pedal is sometimes needed for small hands after the first sixteenth of a beat instead of the second, as at the accented note.

The following general rules may be observed in all cases.

1. In chords, the bass tone must sound as long as the chord does. In wide chords that demand an *arpeggio*-skip, the pedal should be taken with the lowest note, which is played first.

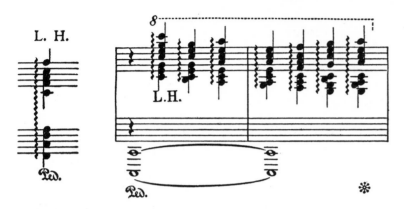

2. The pedal may be more freely employed for high notes than for low or medium positions; because the high tones die away quicker than the low ones, and so are more in need of being sustained. In fairly high positions, therefore, the pedal may be used for actual dissonances, which will not shock the ear as they would in lower octaves. The student may convince himself of this by playing the chromatic scale up and down in the three-lined octave, with pedal throughout.

3. In pedaling, the low bass notes will resound strongly enough to mask higher notes played later. In ascending passages, therefore, low notes held by pedal must be released before playing any notes considerably higher, even if the pedal has to be depressed again after being released, and even though the composer may have made the pedal continuous.

4. For the ear, pedal dissonances may be covered by a *crescendo,* the earlier tones being obliterated by the force of the later notes. The student may prove this to himself by playing an upward diatonic scale, *crescendo,*

crescendo

with pedal, releasing the pedal after the highest and strongest note is reached. The effect is not really dissonant, but has a peculiar style of its own. Chopin used it at the close of his Étude, op. 25, No. 11, where a heavy tonic minor chord at the beginning helps to suggest the idea of a cadence.

With an organ-point, or long-sustained low note, the effect seems comparatively pure even when dissonant chords come on the higher notes, as shown below.

The soft pedal is not merely for symmetry, but is valuable for the veiled quality of tone that it produces. It is useful in *pianissimo* passages, and is of value in ending a *diminuendo* with extreme delicacy. In the latter case it is practically necessary, for an extremely soft tone obtained without it would have less fulness, even though showing the same power at its start.

To link melody-notes, it is often advisable to employ a "false" pedal, used only for short intervals of time. In the above illustrations, from Chopin's *Fantasie*, the dotted lines show where the pedal is to be depressed or released.

XXIV. Hints for Performance

1. Melody

In a general way it is true that the playing of a melody is largely a matter of taste and feeling. However, it will be seen that not every one has the best taste; and like all things spiritual, even the best taste may be hampered by material conditions. The rules for performance, therefore, will not be out of place. They are not to be taken as hindrances to the imagination, but as aids.

1. When two notes of different value are found in succession, the longer note must be played with more force than the shorter, as it is to sound longer. See example from Beethoven's Sonata, op. 10, No. 2.

2. An upward passage is usually *crescendo,* a downward passage *diminuendo.* See example below, **from** Schumann's *"Des Abends."*

When the melody moves up or down by large intervals, the contrast of power may be made more marked.

3. The beats of a measure are accented unequally, the louder notes on the strong beats being most prominent. In 4/4 time the first beat is loudest, the third next, the second still less marked, and the fourth softest.

In 3/4 time the first beat is strongest, and the other two successively weaker.

In 6/8 time, the first beat is strongest, the fourth next, the second and third successively lighter, and the fifth and sixth more so.

4. The directions given by the great composers are to be left unchanged, and shown full respect. This is especially important with Beethoven.

5. Should the first three rules give contradictory directions with regard to any certain note, the majority of rules will serve as guide. Thus in a descending melody a long note may fall on a strong beat. Rule 1 calls for a full tone on a long note; but rule 2 demands a light tone on a descending note. Rule 3 decides the question by calling for a loud note on the strong beat. Thus in the example below, from Leschetizky's "Canzone Toscana," the note marked with an asterisk is to be made loud.

[Editor's Note.—In *"Der Moderne Pianist,"* by Marie Prentner, rule 2 is supplemented by the statement that of two notes the higher is to be the stronger. Another eminently sensible rule given in the same book (see below also) states that when a figure or phrase is repeated, its accent and effect must be made different on each appearance. In *"Die Hand des Pianisten,"* Marie Unschuld von Melasfeld adds as a rule the sugges-

tion that in any case of doubt the pianist should sing the melody, as that procedure will tend to prevent false accents or incorrect groupings.]

There are some exceptions to the above rules.

1. When a short note on a weak beat is tied to a following note, to make a syncopation, the note must be played loud.

2. In playing upward, when the highest note falls on a weak beat it must still be louder than the preceding note; as in the example below (single staff), from Chopin's Impromptu in A-flat.

3. In a downward progression, when a long note falls on a weak beat it should be made louder than the

preceding note; as, for instance, the notes marked with an asterisk in the example above, from Beethoven's C-minor Variations.

4. A short note which is released quickly after a longer one must be soft while either ascending or descending; as in the following, at the right, from Mozart's Fantasie.

Chopin often wrote ascending passages *diminuendo,* with good effect.

The foregoing remarks on melody-playing apply also to phrases and passages (especially important in Chopin's works) and even accompaniment figures. Melodic passages are of course treated thus, or excerpts in which the melody has to be brought out, as in the example below from Chopin's E-minor Concerto.

Non-melodic passages, also, comprising scales or broken

chords, are likewise subject to the rules; as the following, at the right, from Grieg's Concerto.

Even Bach may be shaded. Why should the works of this great master always be subjected to a dry and colorless interpretation? Shading is not necessarily a sign of sentimentality. The latter is more usually a matter of *tempo,* as in an exaggerated or misplaced retard, which too many Chopin-players employ.

One ought not to play several successive tones with exactly the same power; for this brings about a hardness of effect, as if from too great volume of tone. Too great evenness in *piano* work is apt to destroy

the expression; while one may obtain effects of much feeling in *forte* passages by lessening the power of a figure here and there.

Contrast in shading, the repetition of the same phrase with varying power, is also productive of good results. A phrase occurring twice may be played strongly at first, then softly, as an echo; or softly at first, and then more insistently to emphasize it. The style chosen will depend upon the character of the music and the player's taste; or possibly upon the composer's directions, as in the following, from Eduard Schuett's op. 35.

The observance of these general rules should not in the least hamper the freedom of original fancy or emotional expression. One may give full play to these qualities—if he has them.

2. Tempo

If the idea of color is applied to musical dynamics, then *tempo* may be termed the life and movement of piano playing. This should not be the monotonous movement of daily existence, as if timed by a metro-nome.

As variety is the spice of life, according to the proverb, so also constant changes in *tempo* and contrasts in movement will give charm of style.

No composition should be played in a uniform *tempo* from beginning to end. Even in exercises, that should be done only when the student is practising for finger-dexterity alone. In the performance of Études there is room for much taste in style, though here the expression depends chiefly upon the dynamic contrasts.

Changes of *tempo* must be so gradually and delicately managed that the listener will not notice their beginning or end; otherwise the effect would be like a series of sudden jerks. Thus for a *ritardando* the decrease in speed must be calculated accurately, so that the end will not drag; and similarly, in an *accelerando* the pace must not become too fast for the end to seem a climax. In a *ritenuto,* also, many will play the final note at a premature resumption of speed, which robs the hearer of an expected climax. When an *a tempo* follows, it need not always be taken literally at first; it may even be led up to gradually, beginning the new phrase almost like an improvisation. The original *tempo* would be recovered in one or two measures, as in the example at the left.

But whenever the character of the piece demands it, the *a tempo* may be given full speed at once, as below.

A word about the metronome may be in place here. If taken too accurately, it is a stiff pedant without any emotion; but if used in moderation, it is of great advantage. It is really not only a device to measure time, but a good training for evenness and control of rhythm. Every student should use it for the playing of scales, Études, and even pieces. He will then see whether he has been retarding at the hard places, and hurrying at the easy ones.

The exercise at the left will correct such bar-inaccuracy. It can

be played, or merely taken mentally, with quintolets and sextolets *ad lib*.

While these measures are practised in the prescribed succession, and afterward in any order, the pointer of the metronome is to be set at a moderate number and each tick taken as a quarter note.

There is still another reason why it is wise to try over pieces occasionally with the metronome. There may often be found in one piece two themes of different character, both taken at the same *tempo*. One **may** be bright and lively, perhaps, while the other is soft and gentle. Here the metronome will help to keep **the** *tempo* unchanged.

3. Rhythm

Rhythm does not imply an absolutely fixed time for each beat; but within each bar it permits a **fairly free** disposal of beats. Thus individual beats may be lengthened or shortened, the difference being **adjusted**

in other beats; but whole measures may not be changed in proportion to one another. The foregoing **ex-ample** from Schumann's "Grillen" will show (by the asterisks) which notes are to be prolonged.

It is, therefore, a blunder on the part of the pianist to hurry over the end of a measure and begin **the** next one too soon. For this "fever of rhythm" the most useful remedy is the counting of beats or half-beats in slow *tempo*. It is more permissible to retard the beginning of a measure, in case it is accented, or for some special effect.

In the above, from Schumann's "Grillen," the octave marked with an *arpeggio* is to be played with its lower note beginning on time, and its upper note struck an instant later with the chord. This produces a slight retardation, but wholly within the measure.

A slight shortening of the first beat after striking it is allowed in waltzes. The bass note in the **right-hand** example may be accented and the hand carried over to the next beat. The slight abbreviation of the first

beat involves an upward motion of the wrist. The third beat is played on time, but *staccato* and a little lighter. This gives the accompaniment a swingy character, though it will become cheap if overdone.

In the 3/4 rhythm of the Mazurka, the accent may fall on any beat. The first example is from Chopin's op. 7, the other one from Leschetizky's Mazurka. Incidentally, it is said that Chopin never played his own Mazurkas twice alike.

In the accompaniment of a Polonaise, the first beat may be accented, and held a small fraction beyond its due time, the slight retard being taken out of the next two sixteenth-notes. The other beats are normal.

4. Arpeggios

One should not limit his *arpeggios* to those chords that are too wide to be played with one stroke of each hand. The *arpeggio* may be used also when an expressive or emotional effect is desired. In such cases

the right hand may play its chord *arpeggio,* while the left-hand plays "flat," as in the above example from Paderewski's Legende.

On the other hand, the chord sounds more energetic, without becoming hard, if the left hand plays

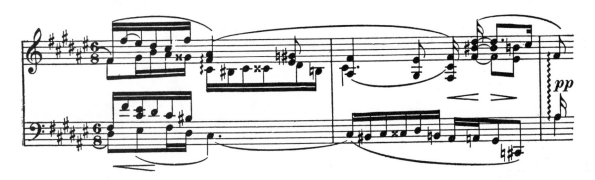

arpeggio and the right hand flat; but the *arpeggio* here must be very swift. The example is from Chopin's Scherzo.

An *arpeggio* may sometimes be used for the purpose of giving a more distinct effect to polyphony at important points, as where one voice ends and another begins, etc. See above in Schumann's Romanze.

The same is true of a canon, as shown in Paderewski's Thème Varié.

The bass tone and the melody note need not be always taken together with rhythmic precision. The latter will have a better effect if played an instant later than the former, even when no *arpeggio* is marked. This can be done at the beginning of a phrase, or on important notes; but the two hands should play together on weak beats. The melody note must come so closely after the other that the pause between them will scarcely be noticed by the hearer, as in the following, from a Chopin Nocturne.

XXV. Fingering

A fingering that is easy may be taken as correct, if the effect of the music is not injured. To play well, the performer needs ease and confidence; and he will do well to decide upon the fingering in advance. The latter cannot always be printed on a piece, because hands of different size and reach will take the same passages differently.

Many rules for fingering have been given in the preceding pages, and to these one more may be added. Loud notes should be played by strong fingers whenever that is possible.

In defiance of all rules, one may sometimes let the fingers run out to the fifth when an under-passing would seem proper. By this means a very rapid *tempo* can be kept up, as in the following from Weber's "Concertstück."

Occasionally the thumb may be under-passed to a black key, when the tone has some accent and the next notes are made easy to reach. This passing must not be done in the usual way, but with a swing of the wrist that will bring the hand up and give the thumb free play. The first example is from Leschetizky's "Cascade."

Another example is found in Rubinstein's fourth Concerto.

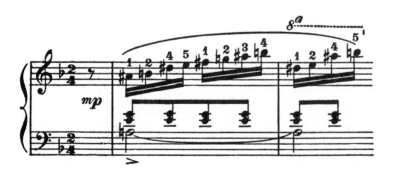

For the most part, any one who has the necessary confidence and courage may go as far as he pleases in adopting irregular fingerings, always providing that they do not interfere with a good performance. Rules, however, must not be broken by mere caprice; there should always be an improvement in effect or facility to justify an irregular fingering. If the given fingering, or that usually adopted, seems good, do not change it, but seek new fingerings suited to special hands only when it proves necessary or advisable.

The pedal is of great assistance in fingering. It links intervals that cannot be stretched by the hand alone, and allows the hand to leave a chord in time to prepare the next one. In melody, too, a tone may be sustained by pedal when hand and finger are needed elsewhere.

XXVI. Practice and Study

Art is a most valued possession of mankind. It cannot be gained by birth or inheritance, but must be attained by the individual. If this were not so, the artist's laurels would be easily won, and of little value. When any one says that he can learn without effort, he is either mistaken, or what he learns will prove of little worth. Only thought can come from the brain without effort; the technique of every art must be gained step by step. How many chisel-blows of preliminary practice were needed before a Venus of Milo could be formed from the rough marble? How many thousand strokes of the brush were made by Raphael in painting his Sistine Madonna? And what pains did he have to take before he could guide the brush so skilfully? Practice makes perfect; and no talent, not even that of a pianist, is injured by practice.

Piano practice should never become a thoughtless throwing-off of exercises by the hour or by the number. To gain good results, it must train head and hand alike. For untrained fingers, even the simplest exercise will demand the utmost attention. The student must notice whether the hand is held properly, and the fingers move correctly; he must listen to each tone, and use thought in every detail. After the fingers have been properly governed by thought for some weeks, he will find that at last they will begin to grow reliable and independent. Then the mental effort may be more fully concentrated on the study of pieces.

Extreme slowness in the early stages of practice will give the student sufficient time to consider every step; and only after he is sure of these steps should he take the exercises more rapidly. If progress is slow at first, it does not follow that the student should sit at the piano all day; such excess would be injurious to the health, and it would not be possible for him to concentrate his attention for such a long period. Four hours of well-considered practice are quite enough. When the player wishes to keep familiar with a large number of pieces, he may spend one or two hours more in such memorizing.

As soon as the student has become proficient in the finger-exercises, scales, and *arpeggios,* they may be practically illustrated by the study of Études. Czerny's *"Schule der Fingerfertigkeit"* ("School of Velocity") should come first, followed by fairly short and easy pieces. The latter may be treated like exercises at first, with each hand by itself, and each part slower and somewhat louder than it will be given in the piece. In Études, the single parts may be taken as quickly as possible, and repeated a number of times for endurance.

Thought is indispensable in the study of pieces, as they are learned first by the brain, and from that by the fingers. Memorizing is important, because by this process a piece is permanently mastered by the brain.

To memorize a piece, read it through at the keyboard only once, to get its outline without creating any faulty habits of fingering. Then take one or two measures at a time, or even more in an easy piece, analyze the harmonies, and decide upon the fingering and pedaling. Study each passage in its proper *tempo,* thus insuring results that are suitable for that *tempo.*

Play the leading sections louder, and the subordinate parts softer; but do not try to put in great expression before the music is learned, as otherwise much feeling may be wasted on a wrong note.

Next read the practised measures through carefully with the eye, and by repeating this, along with the actual naming of the notes, the music will be made to stand out clearly in mental vision. Then, and not before, play the entire phrase or section from memory, taking care to make the speed such that the memory is always able to keep the pace.

If a note is forgotten, it should not be groped for by the fingers, nor should the passage be continued by ear. The student should stop and try to think of the note mentally, looking at the page as a last resort.

When the part of the piece first taken up can be played correctly without hesitation, a second section must be treated in the same way. When later divisions of the piece are learned, they may be played through with the preceding section, and from the beginning. This method is called "memorizing by addition."

If the student finds on the next day that he has forgotten the piece, he should not be discouraged, but may begin as before. This time the piece will come more rapidly, and after some days it will be mastered permanently.

The shading and refining may be taken next; the phrases may be given due expression, and the contrasts properly distributed. In the dynamics and phrasing, proceed step by step, taking a convenient part at a time, as in memorizing.

A piece learned by this method is not easily forgotten, even though played very infrequently; and neither memory nor fingers are apt to fail, as they may do if one relies too much on the latter. For the finger-devotee, brain-study will come hard at first, and may be increased very gradually, with periods of rest. Such pauses may be devoted to finger-exercises, or to some occupation apart from the piano. At last one will be able to think fast enough to keep the fingers always busy.

According to Leschetizky, "Learning by this method seems slow, but is really quick enough. By taking even a few lines daily at first, and not more than a page a day later on, and counting only two-thirds of a year for work, one may nevertheless learn over two hundred pages a year, not including perhaps half as many more that come as repetitions in the pieces. Thus in the first year a respectable number of pieces will be learned, and the routine of later years will double or treble this number." The same method is advisable even for those students whose ability enables them to play a piece from memory after merely glancing through it. For these the method will not prove hard, and it will insure correctness in recitals. The performer should be a different person on the concert platform from what he is at home. In the former position, he loses a part of his surety; and in consequence he can never have too much of this valuable quality. The student should therefore make it a point to play his pieces correctly from beginning to end immediately after finishing the piecemeal study of them. Playing correctly after several trials does not imply great accuracy. If the student does break down, he should pause for a time and then begin over afterward, as if for a new "first trial." The same method applies to Études, or to pieces already memorized. At the piano, the performer must think only of what he is playing, no matter how much he imagines he has mastered it. Thought is the safest guide for avoiding mistakes; it is like reins for the fingers, guiding them in the right road.

Self-criticism is a further step in correct playing. He who can criticise his own work as keenly as he would that of another, is well advanced. The ability to recognize one's own faults means much, although it requires still further effort to correct them.

Even those pianists who prefer not to give concerts, but who play "merely for their own enjoyment," should adopt proper methods; unless this, perhaps, will lessen "their own enjoyment." They should try, in any case, if only from selfish motives; for every one is pleased to show ability, even for a small audience. We might have been forced to hear deliberately poor work, had not a kind Providence provided "stage-fright." The true artist finds this an obstacle to be overcome only by continued study, and by frequent playing in public, to gain confidence. But it is also a spur to better work. Like the hero of Schiller's "Fight with the Dragon," who first used a painted dragon to lessen his horse's fright of the real one, the performer may diminish his fear of the public by playing for many people in private. He may hunt for a kindly hearing everywhere. When he reaches the stage, too, he may play for his fellow-artists; for if he can satisfy their standards, he will surely conquer his dragon.

XXVII. Hand and Arm Movement

Some pianists of exuberant temperament execute athletic "stunts" with their hands raised, as if to show that they are above physical limitations, and make sport of all difficulties. These fancy tricks have their measure of effect, and may be condoned when the performance is good. On the other hand, there are certain necessary movements of the wrist, which aid in phrasing, or help the rhythm, or rest the hand after the effort of strong chord-playing. There are also arm motions, such as the natural rising after strong notes. All these movements should have grace and freedom.

The necessary hand and arm movements vary in different pieces. It is not to be inferred that the fingers should gambol merrily in a scherzo, or glide along sleepily in a Berceuse; but their movements result

from the tone quality obtained. Thus in forcible passages the arm is often raised abruptly, while in soft or melancholy phrases the arm may be lifted more slowly, preferably as little as necessary for the wrist action.

The upward, downward, and rotating movements of the wrist have been already described. Here it is necessary to mention only the sidewise motion that is often needed to bring the hand into position for further playing.

In the above example, from Chopin's Étude, op. 25, No. 1, the melody note E-flat can be taken more easily, and made more expressive, by turning the right hand sidewise a little. The left hand also may be turned in following the accompaniment figure.

Gifted students will find instinctively the proper duty of the wrist, and its relation to the changing position of the hand. Others will have to get this by study, in a sort of preparatory technique for fluent and easy execution.

The pedal is useful here also. By sustaining the notes, it leaves the hand free to assume its next position, as at the starred chords in the following, from Chopin's Fantaisie.

The subject of preparatory technique may include also a device to aid in obtaining a clean-cut bass. This is not so generally clean-cut as might be thought, as is shown by Liszt's term "pseudo-basses." The trouble usually arises from the fact that skips or difficult passages in the right hand often distract attention from the left. The device consists of touching the octave above the bass note with the left thumb (though of course

not playing it). The little finger can strike the actual note easily enough, as practically every one can stretch an octave. This device may be practised without looking at the left hand.

Another point that may be mentioned here concerns large skips, which are often a source of trouble. Practice alone will not give certainty, but presence of mind is required, and control of methods. The following procedure will be found helpful.

For a skip on the white keys, the hand should not rise in a high curve, but should glide rapidly along the edge of the keyboard, allowing the little finger to strike the proper note with its outer edge instead of its tip. The wrist must be lowered at the same time. This method avoids the disadvantage of hiding the key from the eye. It is also of use to name the note mentally when ready to strike it.

For a skip to a black key, the hand is again kept near the keyboard; but here the finger, preferably the third, strikes in a flattened position with its tip, instead of with its edge. The wrist cannot well be lowered here, but it must not be raised too high.

The many rules for the use of finger and hand should not discourage the student. These rules finally give the fingers a most delicate sensibility, and enable the wrist to aid and follow them perfectly. The arm, however, usually remains a "clumsy fellow," requiring much guidance to prevent its interfering with correct wrist and finger movements. For this reason, even in the earliest scale and *arpeggio* practice, the student must not let it move out too rapidly or sag back awkwardly.

XXVIII. Who Should Study Piano?

The title of this section forms a very delicate question. I fear very much that a short and sharp reply from the world would say, "No one." But that would be wrong, if only because of the rich and varied repertoire of the piano, which needs an unbroken series of interpreters. But these interpreters must "have a calling"; and that gives the reply to the question. Only those who are properly gifted and impelled by native ability and fitness should become public pianists.

What qualities satisfy this standard? If I said, "Only talent of the highest order," I might just as well claim that only millionaires have the right to live. In music, as in life, there must be a middle class.

To become a thorough pianist, one must have a good ear, a suitable hand, artistic temperament, real sensibility, brains, and unceasing industry.

The musical ear varies decidedly in degree. Best of all is the one that has "absolute pitch," and can recognize any tone, whether given by instrument or not. Next comes the ability to recognize comparative pitch, and tell any interval from a given note. This sort of ear is more usual, and capable of real development. Musicians who possess it (as all good ones should) often show a refined sense of shading. The lowest grade of ear for the student would merely enable him to repeat correctly a tone that he hears.

An inferior ear may be improved by a certain kind of singing exercise; not for vocal proficiency, but merely for pitch. Sing a natural and easy tone, find its pitch on the piano, and grow familiar with it. Then play this tone, and at the same time sing definite intervals above and below it, repeating each interval until it becomes accurate. Also try to name intervals and chords played by some other person at the piano. If these exercises are practised fifteen minutes daily, progress will be made.

Regarding the hand, some statements were made in Section II. Here it may be added that even an imperfectly adapted hand will be changed by faithful and intelligent practice into a real "piano-hand," suitable for the requirements of performance.

[EDITOR'S NOTE.—A small hand may be gradually stretched to manage larger intervals by the careful use of proper exercises, and an equally careful avoidance of over-exertion. These exercises consist of playing paired notes with each pair of fingers, beginning with the adjacent ones and giving them most of the time. Start in each case with a semitone, and play increasing chromatic intervals (repeating one of the notes) until their size is as great as can be handled without strain. It is also of use to play the fixed note while holding the other, and *vice versa*.]

Unlike the hand, the temperament cannot be altered. A phlegmatic student may have all other good qualities, and still be a constant worry to his teacher and a failure in moving the public. A surplus of temperament is better than a lack of it, as it can be restrained, but not created. A player without temperament will show an absence of emotion in his performances. Emotion cannot be manufactured, but merely refined, or awakened if dormant.

But musicians themselves should combat the idea that music needs only feeling and emotion, without brains and intelligence. The latter are necessary, not merely to hide a possible defect in achievement, but to give even a moderately worthy interpretation of all pieces except the most valueless musical trifles.

But however great one's talent may be, he can reach a greater height by industry with little talent than by talent with little industry. Faithful and persistent work will help the student over many hard places; but even marked natural gifts, without work, will degenerate. In fact, the distant summit of Parnassus can be attained only with the aid of the double team, Industry and Talent.

APPENDIX

1. SCALE OF SCALES, SCALE OF ARPEGGIOS, AND SERIES OF ARPEGGIOS

The following systematic grouping of scales and *arpeggios* should not be started until the student has mastered the ordinary scales and broken chords in rapid and even execution. The following sets need great endurance, for each one is to be played entire, without interruption. The connecting fingering is given. The endurance, however, should be acquired gradually, and excessive fatigue should be avoided by not overdoing these exercises. They may be played through once a day, which will not only maintain technical ability, but increase it.

SCALE OF SCALES

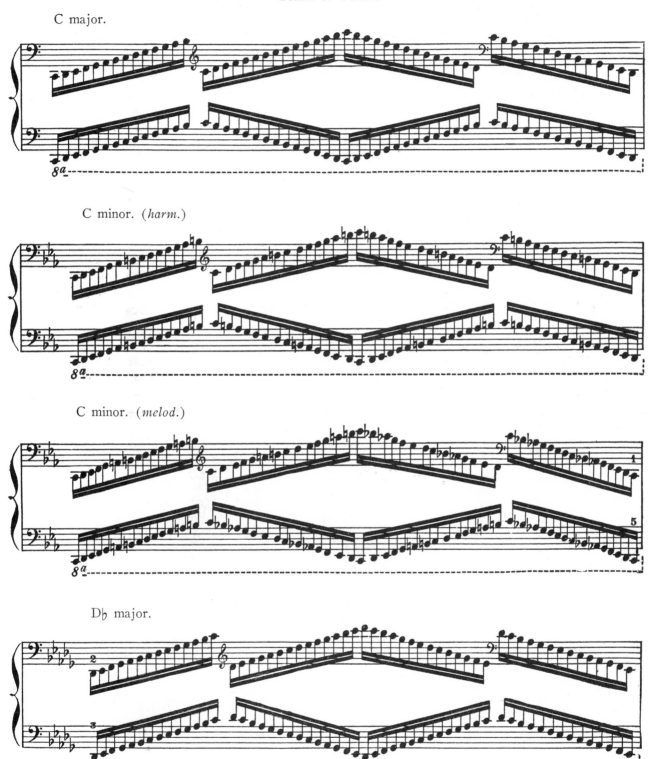

C♯ minor. (*harm.*)

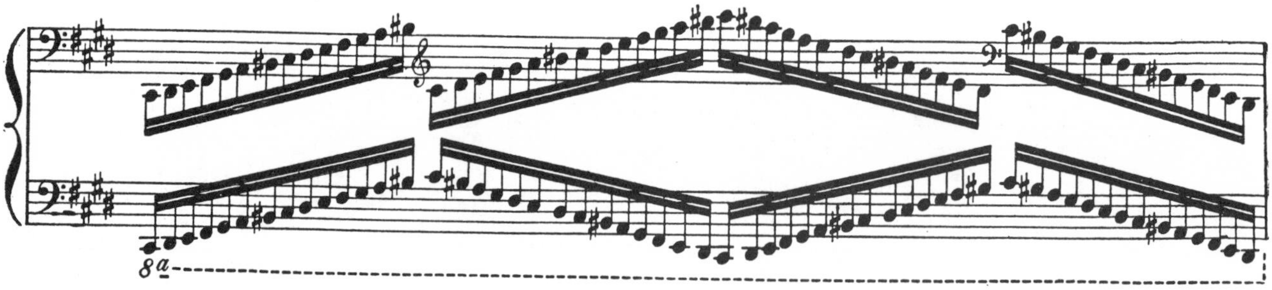

C♯ minor. (*melod.*)

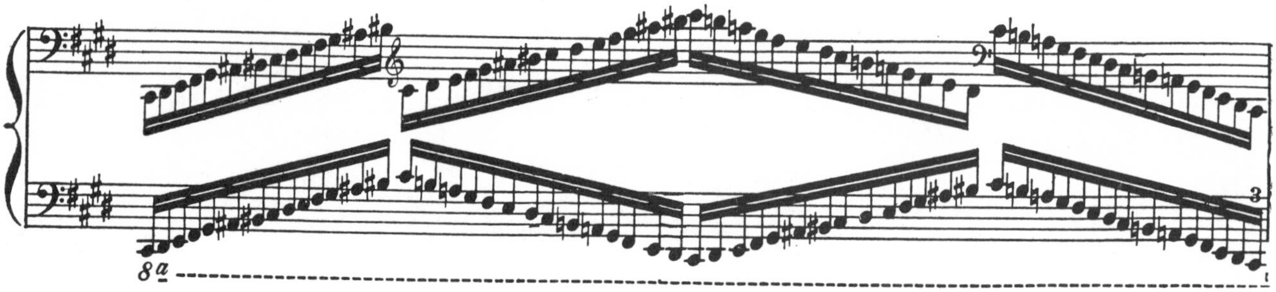

D major.

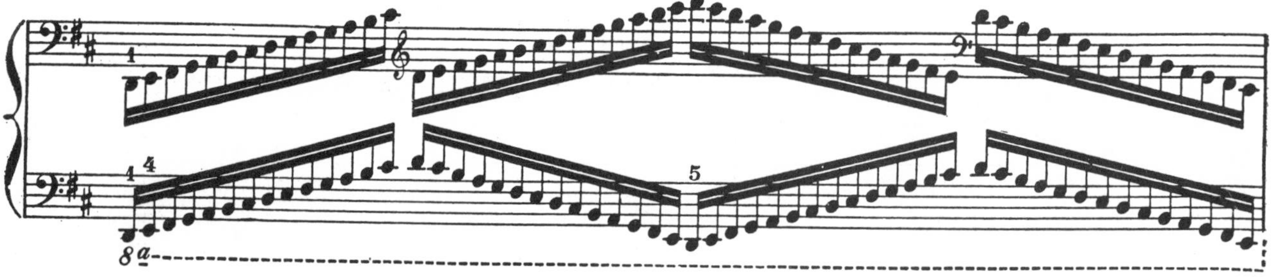

D minor. (*harm.*)

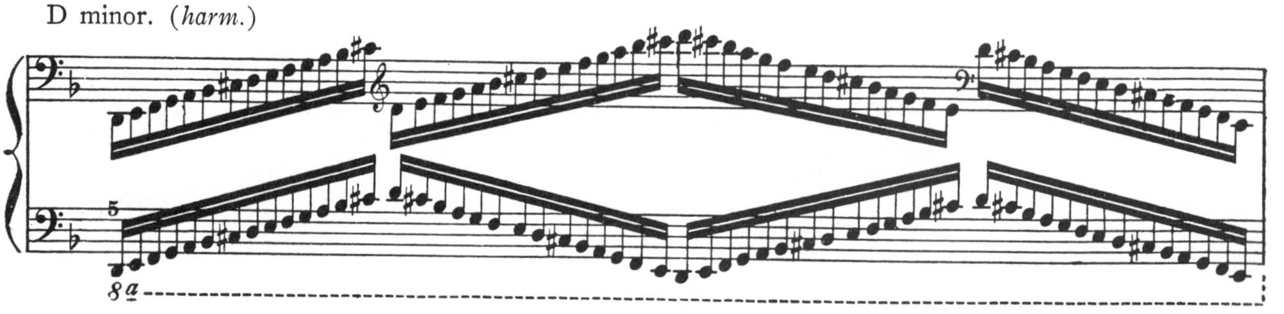

D minor. (*melod.*)

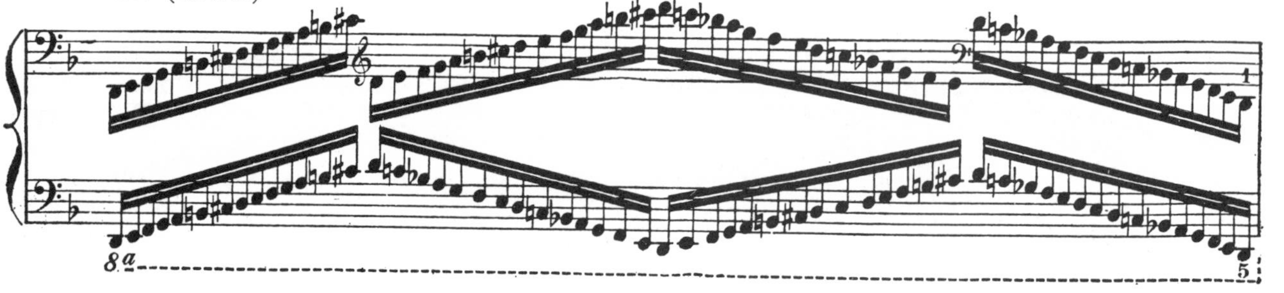

Eb major.

Eb minor. (*harm.*)

Eb minor. (*melod.*)

E major.

E minor. (*harm.*)

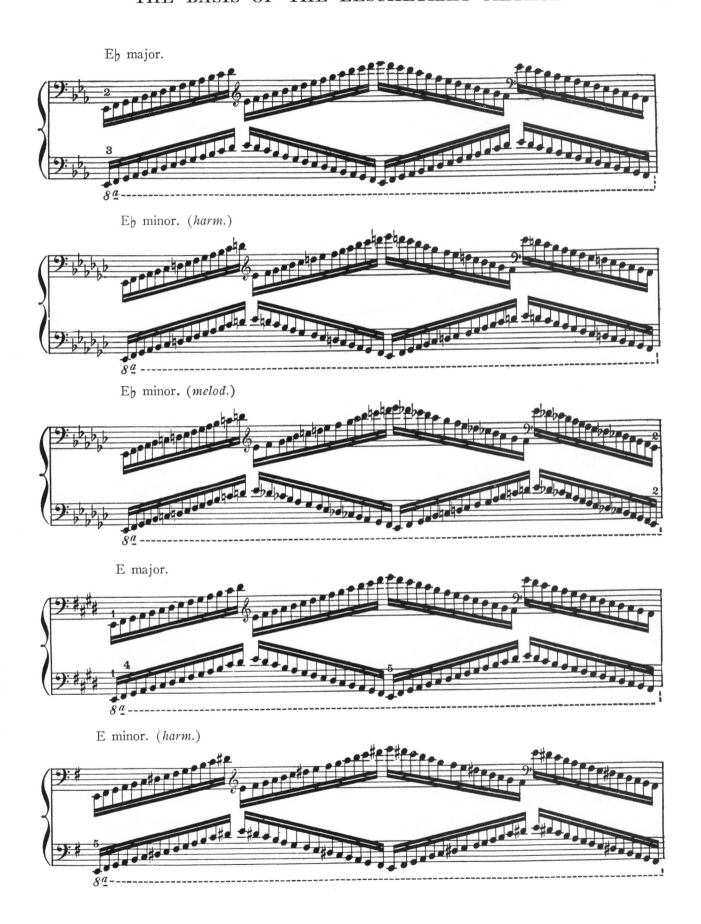

E minor. (*melod.*)

F major.

F minor. (*harm.*)

F minor. (*melod.*)

F♯ major.

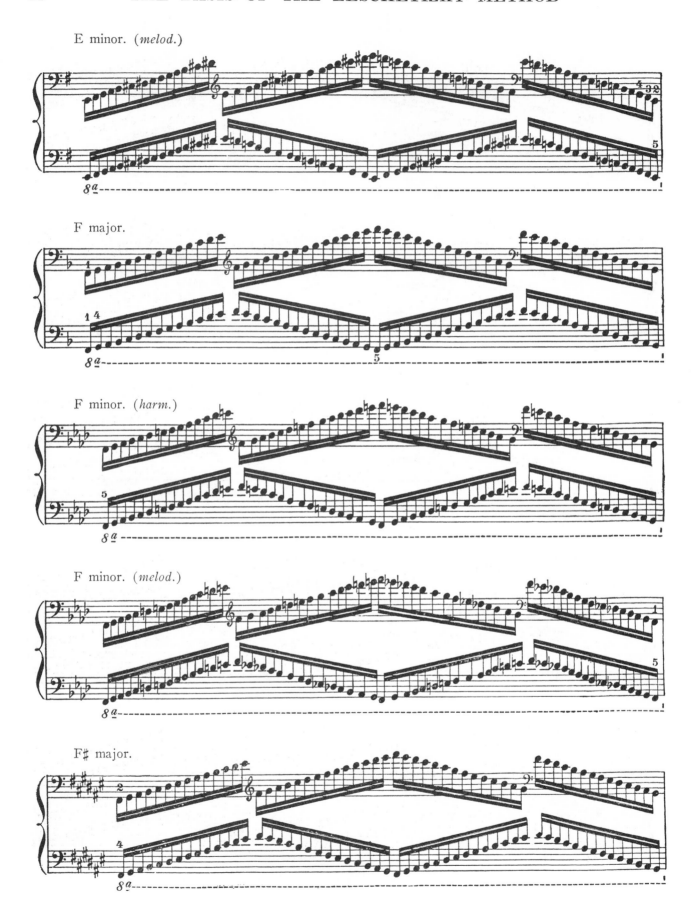

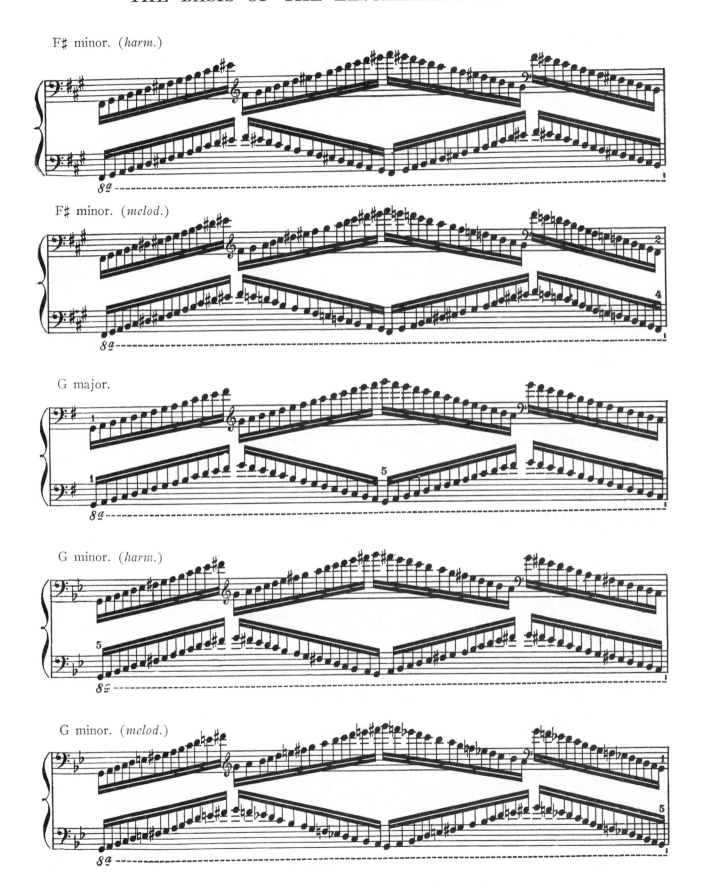

Ab major.

G♯ minor. (*harm.*)

G♯ minor. (*melod.*)

A major.

A minor. (*harm.*)

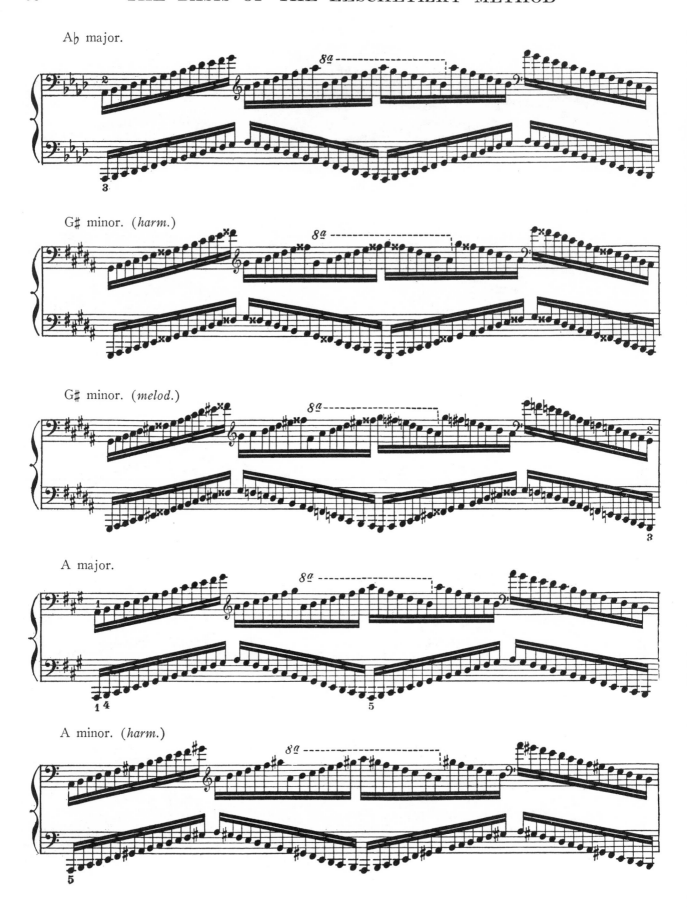

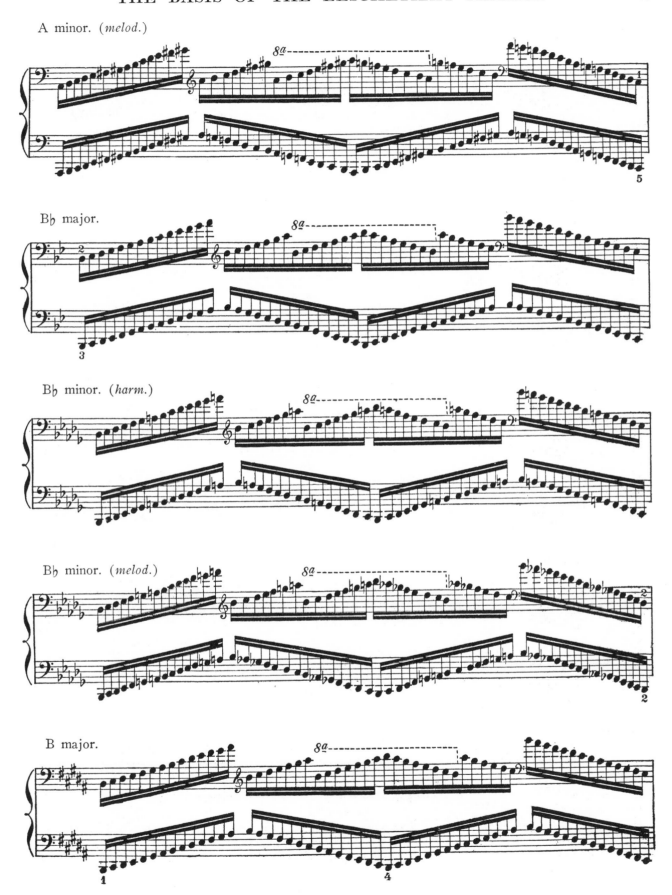

B minor. (*harm.*)

B minor (*melod.*)

Chromatic.

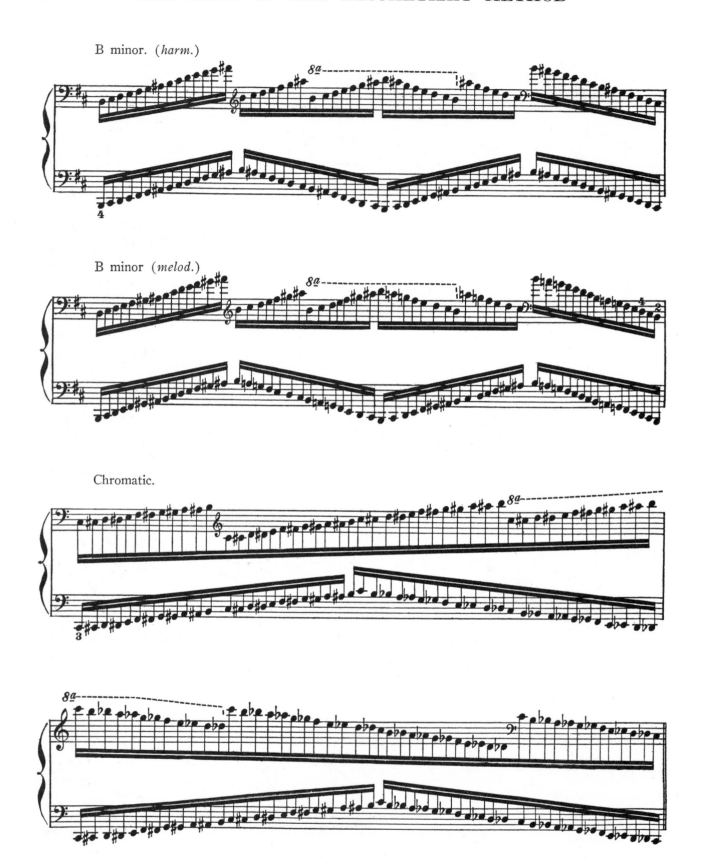

Scale of Arpeggios

Practise with both the fingerings given. Take the keynote, whenever it occurs, always with the regular fingering (that closest to the heads of the notes).

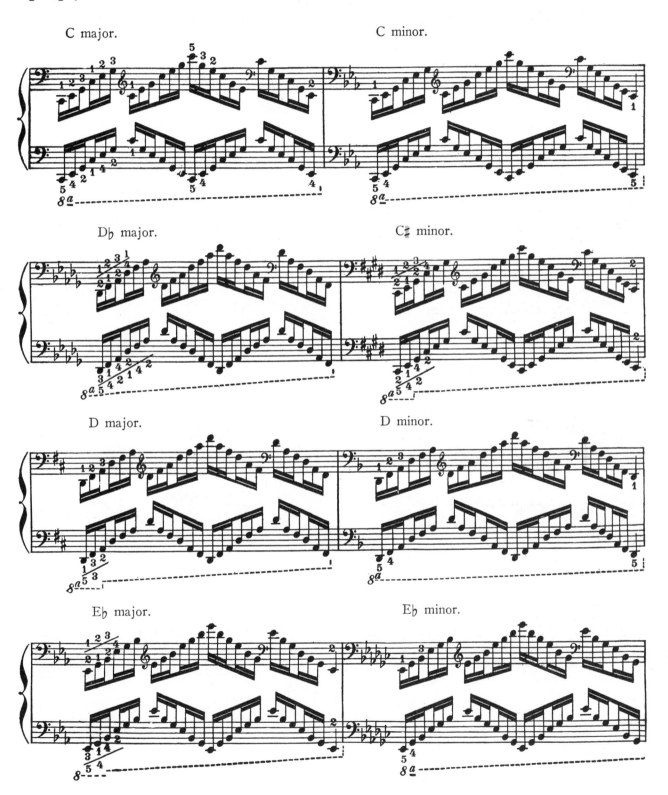

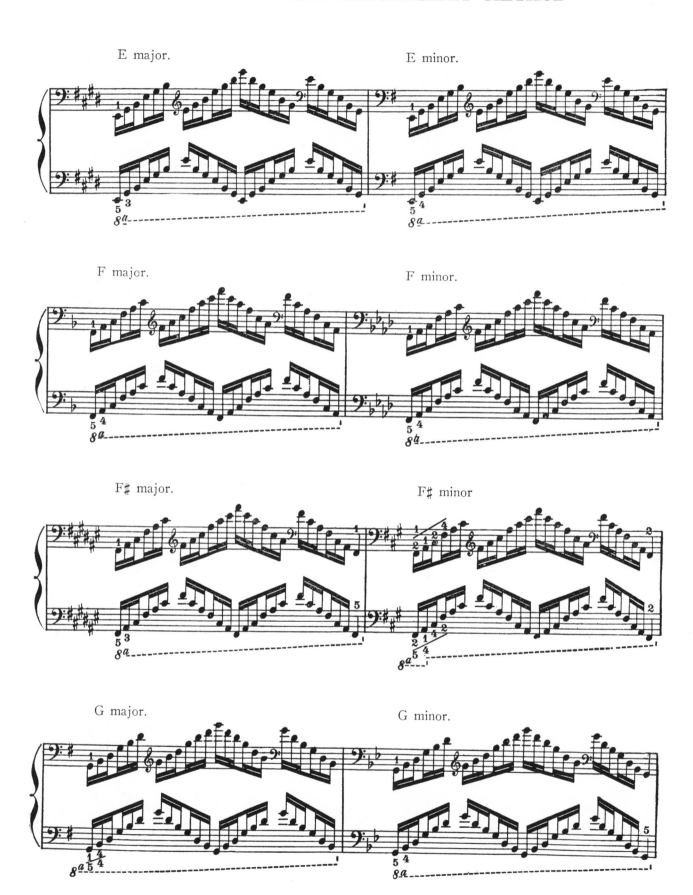

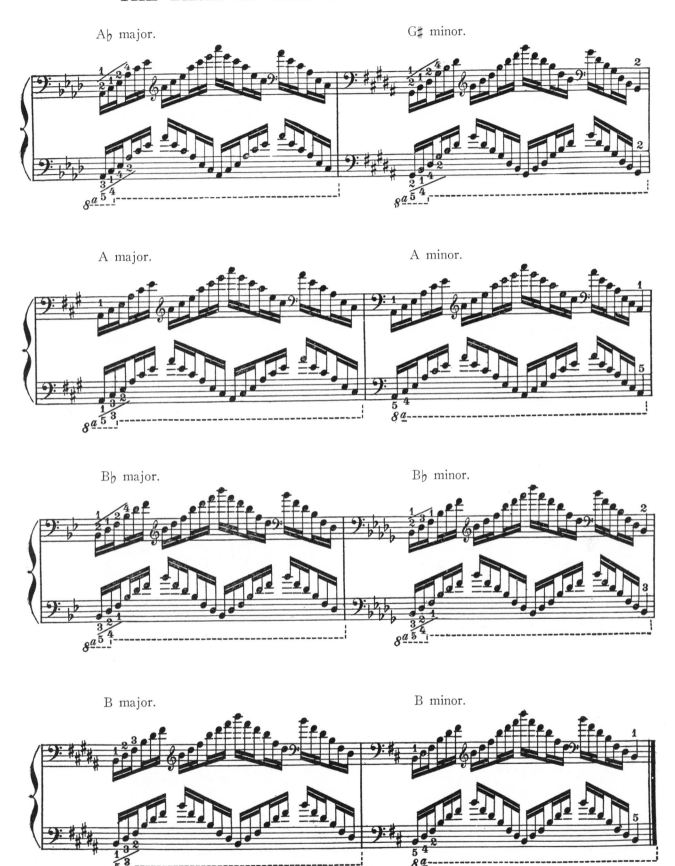

SERIES OF ARPEGGIOS

TRIADS AND SEVENTH CHORDS

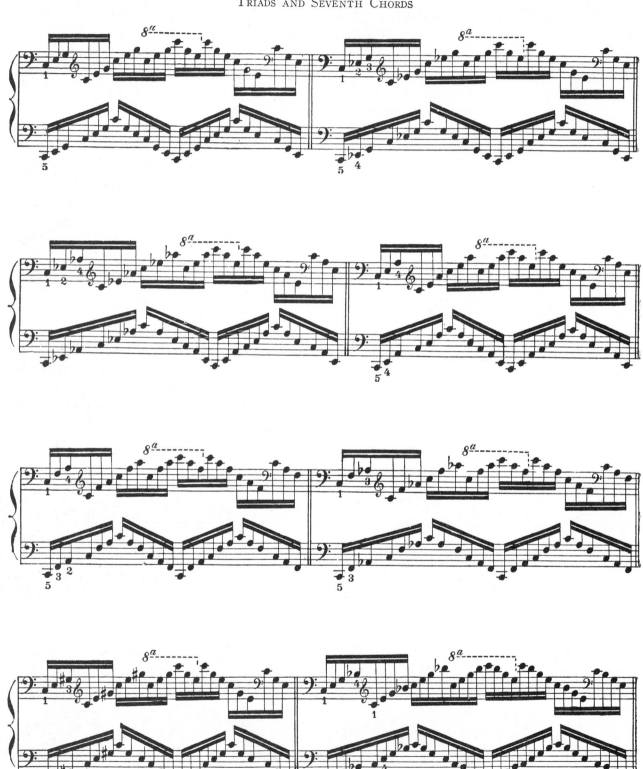

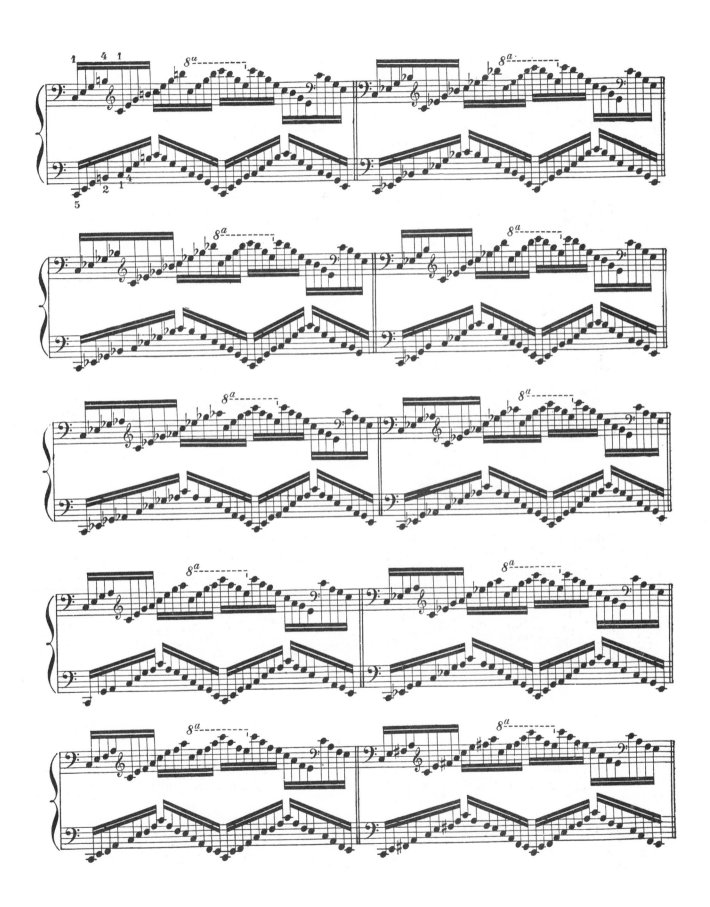

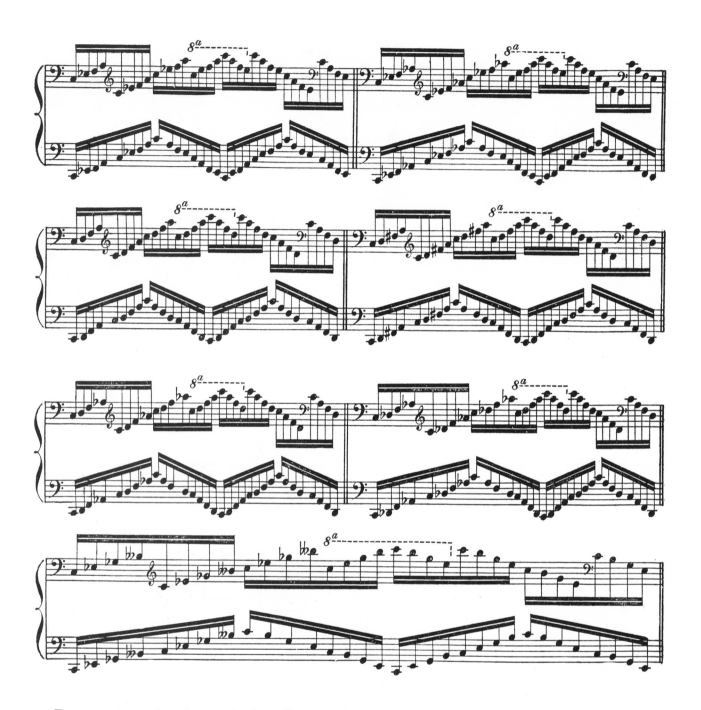

Transpose tne series of *arpeggios* into all keys, using only the regular fingering, as in the following illustrations.

CONCLUSION

The basis of the Leschetizky Method is intended largely for piano-players who have had more than a beginner's training. This does not, however, prevent beginners from using it, or even children, if they follow the method faithfully. They should first, however, receive some elementary training in Theory and Notation. Then from the instant they set their hands on the keyboard they should be guided by the rules given in this book. Children, of course, should not play exercises for as long a time per day as adults, nor should they be made to attempt intervals suited only to adults.

Pianists who try to rebuild their method in accordance with that of Leschetizky will succeed only by abstaining entirely from their old style while forming the new one. They will even have to give up reading at sight. The change must be regarded as a method of "treatment," during which the prescribed diet must be strictly adhered to; and any indulgence in forbidden fruit would cause much loss of time. Even after the pianist has fully mastered his exercises and scales in the new method, it will be wise for him to omit his former repertoire of pieces for a time, taking up new Études and compositions, and not playing any of the old ones until there is no danger of their causing a return to former faults of method.

The pianist need not fear that he will lose his former dexterity by this second start. It will return afterward with more power and perfection than ever.

He who changes his method in this manner will need patience, and again patience; but he will be repaid by the result, which has converted many a skeptic.

EXERCISES WITHOUT KEYBOARD

By CLEMENT ANTROBUS HARRIS

T is not sufficiently known that no weight, no keyboard, no apparatus whatever, is necessary for the preliminary training of either fingers or wrist for pianoforte playing! Indeed, in the case of very young children or older pupils with exceptionally weak fingers, the keyboard is better avoided. There is no excuse for overworking the muscles, for nothing in the nature of strain is ever necessary. The idea that the lifting of heavy weights or some other form of strenuous resistance is necessary to muscular development is happily exploded. Hence the substitution in the drill hall of light wooden dumb-bells for the heavy iron ones used by our fathers. All that is needed is care that the right muscles are being brought into play, and frequent but short practices.

FIG. 1.

It is said that Sir Michael Costa's arm was as strong as that of a blacksmith. Yet he never wielded anything heavier than an ebony baton! It was the frequency of his arm action, not the weight he lifted, which made a modern Cyclops of him. It is not the muscles which bring the fingers down which are so weak and sluggish: these are developed in every-day life; it is the muscles which raise the fingers. And the training of these needs no resistance beyond that afforded by the weight of the fingers to be raised.

Let the hand and arm be placed upon a table, with the hand in correct position for playing: the fingers well rounded, and the thumb lying flat, so that the tip of the index, or second finger, is nearly in line with the nail of the thumb, as in Fig. 1 above. Then exercise each finger in turn, raising it, say, ten times

FIG. 2.

successively. Next, to attain independence, raise the fingers once each in various orders of succession, such as 1, 3, 2, 4, 3, 5, until considerable rapidity and

freedom are gained. Following this, a book of five-finger exercises may be used and played upon the table instead of the piano.

Wrist exercises should be done in a similar manner. Place the arm on the table as before, but with the wrist hanging over the edge. Then alternately raise and depress the hand, taking care that it pivots at the wrist, and that the arm remains stationary, as in Fig. 2.

When wrist action is taught at the keyboard, care should be taken that it is used in producing the impact

FIG. 3.

of the hand on the note, and not merely in raising the hand *after* playing the note. A spurious wrist action is not uncommon, in which the note is played by finger touch and the hand is then raised by wrist action; it is then brought down by wrist action, but as it reaches the keys its motion is arrested and finger action is substituted, so that wrist touch never really takes place. To cure this the teacher must insist that the hand be raised *before the first note is played* and allowed to fall direct on to the keys *without the intervention of finger touch*.

If the attention is allowed to flag during wrist exercises the hand will be raised less and less, until at last it is hardly raised at all. Needless to say, it should be raised until the palm is nearly at right angles to the forearm. To insure this, it will be found useful in the case of young pupils for the teacher to take hold lightly of the pupil's wrist, raise his

FIG. 4.

—the teacher's—index finger, and instruct the pupil to raise his hand until the knuckles touch the teacher's finger. Elder pupils do not, of course, like to be superintended quite so closely. A diagram will make the plan clear. See Fig. 3.

To the ordinary wrist exercises occasional practice of rotary motion should be added. All that is necessary is for the forearm to be turned halfway round —which is all that it will go—and back again a few times in succession. The movement is similar to that involved in turning a screw-driver, or winding a clock. See Fig. 4. The passing of the thumb under the fingers; an octave when played tremolo by one hand; a sustained note accompanied by repeated chords in the same hand, and other passages in pianoforte playing, involve a slight rotatory motion of the forearm, and the exercises suggested will greatly facilitate them.

Of finger exercises without apparatus, one of the most useful is simply to move the four fingers (2, 3,

FIG. 5.

4, and 5) to and fro, keeping the thumb and wrist stationary. This, in the case of unpracticed hands, will soon make the fingers ache,—a sure sign that the exercise is needed. It must, of course, be discontinued when the aching begins. It will assist in keeping the hand stationary if, when exercising the fingers of the right hand, those of the left are pressed against the palm of the right hand, and *vice versa.* See Fig. 5.

The idea that pianoforte playing depends solely on finger muscles is now largely discredited. Keyboard exercises, though not displaced, are now supplemented by gymnastics, not only for fingers and wrist, but under some systems for the arm. Several primers have been issued devoted to this aspect of pianoforte technic alone. One of the first was Ward Jackson's *Gymnastics for Fingers and Wrist,* published in England by Metzler & Co. in 1874. A more recent one is *Hand Gymnastics,* by Mr. Ridley Prentice (Novello); but the most elaborate course of such exercises is undoubtedly that prescribed in the *Foundation Exercises* of the Virgil Clavier School.

No recommendation of exercises away from the keyboard would be complete which did not refer to the immense saving of time which they may be made to effect. There are countless odd moments of time when keyboard practice is impossible, but an exercise without apparatus is not. All these may be utilized by the player acquainted with a few exercises in the calisthenics of finger and wrist. Instead of idly "twirling his thumb" he will be turning his time to excellent account; and he will obtain excellent results from comparatively slight efforts.

OTHER PIANO METHODS

By ARTHUR ELSON

N the days when the Leschetizky method has become famous through such players as Paderewski among the men, or Katharine Goodson among the women, one might think that this popular method had displaced all the others. Such, however, is not the fact. A number of methods flourish. Very often, too, the successful teacher will blend different points from two or three, and practically create a new one of his own.

One might also assume that a point of such importance as the position of the hand had been thoroughly settled by the many great pianists of the last century and a half. This, too, would be a mistake. It may slope up or down from the wrist, or be level; while varying degrees of bend in the finger are also called for. In the "Art of Teaching Pianoforte Playing," by J. Alfred Johnstone, that well-known English teacher and writer grows sarcastic over the many varieties of piano touch that are now called for. He mentions the "finger-elastic touch," the "up-arm sweeping touch," the "elastic-fist touch," the "stab touch," the "low-wrist touch," and even the "finger-lying-on-the-keys touch." The last is our old friend, the prepared touch of the Leschetizky method.

With all this variety, it has been thought proper to include here the chief points of two or three of these varying methods. Therefore the method spoken of above (by Johnstone) will be described, as well as the Deppe method and its later development by Breithaupt. It will be noted that in many points the first is practically a direct contradiction of the others. Under the circumstances, teachers are naturally free to "choose the one that they love best," as the juvenile games have it. But an effort will be made here to institute some of those odious things called comparisons.

Incidentally, Johnstone begins with a protest against those who neglect exercises because they want to learn "only enough to amuse their friends." This he calls analogous to a student who slights grammar and spelling because he merely wishes to read and speak a little for his friends, and does not care to become a famous orator or writer. This is a well-chosen point; for it is certainly wise for the student to work in the proper way, no matter what he intends to do in the future.

The objects of finger-training, Johnstone says, are to produce the greatest possible power, independence, delicacy, rapidity, and accuracy in the fingers and their motions. They must also be accustomed to certain musical figures and sets of notes that occur frequently. In doing this, the utmost mental attention is needed. Johnstone, like all other good teachers, realizes the value of thought; and the pupil must always be made to do the same. Exercises are to be played with strict attention to every detail of hand and finger motion, power, and even expression. Not a single movement should be made without having a reason for it. This general principle Johnstone puts in these words: "Never move a finger without knowing exactly how it should be moved, without having a definite intention in your mind, or without doing your utmost to direct that movement so as to gain from it the maximum result possible."

For the position of the hand, some advise a high wrist, and others a low wrist; some insist on a hollow back of the knuckles, while others wish them to form a ridge; again, some insist on fingers raised as high as possible, while others wish them laid on the keys. Johnstone suggests the following experiment, to determine the best position. Lay the hand flat on a table, while sitting close to it. Bend the fingers by curving the joint next the tip slightly, the next joint more, and the knuckles slightly. Then raise the wrist to a level position, the hand resting on the finger-tips and the side of the thumb. With the other hand, lift the middle finger by its outer joint, keeping its curved position; and after the finger is raised, let it drop suddenly, and aid its fall by all the muscular force that can be exerted by the finger alone. The result will be a fairly forcible blow on the table. Now move the hand until the wrist is outside the edge of the table, lower it to a level with that edge, and then repeat the preceding action. Try again with a position like the first case, but with knuckles depressed to make a hollow in the back of the hand. Try the experiment still once more, with the knuckles raised high. Compare the force of the blow in the various cases, and it will be pretty clearly evident that the first position here described will give the best results. A lowered wrist gets a diagonal blow, less powerful than a vertical one. Depressed knuckles prevent the finger from being raised to the proper height. Raised knuckles force the fingers to reach so far down in striking that they lose power. What Johnstone says of the relaxed fingers laid on the keys is quoted later, in connection with the Breithaupt method.

With regard to the comparative merits of striking or pushing the keys, the former is advocated. The supporters of the latter say that all levers should be pushed, and use the oar of a rowboat as an illustration. But the simile is hardly accurate, as the row-boat is a mass to be moved steadily, while a piano-key is a lever that must produce a quick blow with the hammer at its farther end. Johnstone uses the type-writer keys as a much more accurate simile.

Johnstone therefore advises a hand position in which the forearm and wrist form a line sloping slightly toward the keys, and the fingers are curved as described in the first position of his experiment. He notes that weak and inexperienced hands usually tend to lean over toward the little finger, and he calls for a special effort to make the hand slope the other way, so that a marble on the back of either hand would roll off toward the other. He does not, however, give any device to help this. Such a device will be found in a note on the Leschetizky method (this volume), in which the skipping of a key between the second and third fingers is shown to aid in the desired result.

In action, Johnstone suggests the following:

1. The striking finger must be raised rapidly and with great force, pivoting on the knuckle.
2. It should be held in this position, remaining raised with as great force as possible.
3. It should strike with the utmost force and rapidity, depressing the key firmly to the very bottom, while at the same time the finger to be used next should rise with an equal force to an equal height.
4. Finger-tips must not move in and out; there must be no involuntary motion; and no finger should drop at all before starting its striking motion, which is a sudden rush to the key.
5. The nail should not be allowed to strike the key, and the finger-tips should form a curved row, with that of the third finger nearest the line of the black keys.
6. The thumb has its joint bent somewhat, and touches the keys with its side.

The teacher is then advised to keep constant care that the pupil holds the finger firmly in its highest position, and does not let it sag before the time for it to play its note. Evenness of tone and perfect legato are also insisted upon, and a thorough mental attention and concentration. A firm touch is also advised, with each key depressed fully to the bottom, even when playing in soft passages.

Johnstone's finger exercises are begun by a slow trill, and the exercises are arranged for two fingers first, then three, and then five. He does not seem to adopt the single-note exercises of Leschetizky. This seems an error at first sight, but it may not be a fatal one. While the Leschetizky method is undoubtedly justly famous at present, it does not follow that every minute point in the method is far ahead of similar points in other methods. In beginning with two fingers, it will be found that each supports and relieves the other, and that two notes give the beginner a suggestion that he is playing an actual progression, however simple. Johnstone omits the single-finger training in his book, with the exception given

below, but there is no reason why it should not come after the other exercises. But whatever is done first, the teacher must be sure that hand and finger action are begun in the proper way—at least, according to his method.

The slow trill of two notes is repeated thirty to forty times with each pair of fingers, at a metronome rate of 40 to 60 for each note. The trill is taken at its slowest at first, and it is even practicable to let the student rest a beat between each note for a time. This waiting, according to Johnstone, is to be done with the finger on the key just struck, but all other fingers held up as hard as possible. Care must be taken to make the fourth and fifth fingers move as freely as possible. He states, "Unless the little finger be made to move freely at its root joint, and independently of any hand movement, the finger technique will never be clear, brilliant, or accurate." To develop this finger, he advises holding down the other four notes and playing the fifth note with the little finger fifty times in succession, with careful attention to all details.

The slow trill is to be practised continually, with the metronome mark raised in later lessons until 96 is reached. The slow trill with each pair of adjacent fingers may then be taken through all keys that offer new finger-combinations of black and white keys. As the pupil grows more and more proficient, he may take double notes or triplets, with each beat, then with each half-beat, and so on. But speed should never be increased unless the movements are kept correct. The exercises should be practised at each new speed until some improvement is noted, before increasing the pace. All black and white key-combinations are to be used here also. As always, the mind must be concentrated upon each motion.

The foregoing are advised for a year. They may then be changed for a two-note exercise on intervals varying by semitones from a minor second to a major third, and the same taken on each successive note of the chromatic scale without stopping. When played with any force, it will be found so tiring that after one pair of fingers has gone through it, a pair from the other hand (playing downward with the left hand) should be used for relief.

After a year or two the pupil is advised to take the first exercise in double notes, adding a third above the first note in each key.

The next two exercises consist of two successive notes giving a second or a third, the two notes being repeated continually on the next scale-degree instead of on the same one. They are to be taken through a compass of three octaves, ascending and descending three times without stopping. This may be started with a metronome of 72 for each pair of notes, and quickened until four notes can be played to a beat at 144. The exercises are of course played in every key. Care must be taken to have the tone derived wholly from the finger motion, at all speeds. For the sake of practising contractions, the exercise in seconds may be taken by all possible combinations of fingers not adjacent—1-3, 1-4, 1-5, 2-4, 2-5, 3-5.

In all these the student is directed to make half of his practice a succession of slow notes played with rapid finger-motion after each finger has been held high. Continual practice at high speed is not advisable, even for the advanced student. He may play each exercise twice at a slow rate, with full uplift of fingers and forcible stroke; and then twice at double the speed, after he has mastered the latter point.

The three-finger exercises are devoted largely to the strengthening of the weak fourth and fifth fingers, in combination with their more powerful neighbor, the third. Johnstone suggests them for more earnest students, while considering the first few two-finger exercises necessary for all, whether they wish to become advanced or not. The same directions as before apply to these new exercises, and special care must be taken to give strength to the stroke of the fourth finger. Four exercises are given. The first consists of three notes in succession, played with the fingering 3, 4, 5, and repeated on successively higher or lower scale degrees through three octaves. The second consists of the triplet E, D, E, repeated on successively higher and lower degrees through three octaves. The fingering here is 4, 3, 4 on the first triplet, 5, 3, 4 on the others going upward, and 4, 3, 5 coming down with the right hand. The left hand has 4, 5, 4 on the first triplet, 3, 5, 4 on the others going up, and 4, 5, 3 coming down. A third exercise starts, let us say, with C, D, C, and the fingering of the two hands in the previous exercise is exchanged for this. A fourth consists of four notes to the beat, arranged to proceed gradually upward. They may all be carried through three octaves up and down, and repeated three times before changing hands. A fifth exercise consists of holding down an octave with thumb and little finger, and playing the intervening notes of the dominant seventh chord as a broken chord repeated, both upward and downward. This is claimed as an aid for increasing the reach. The three inversions of the chord may be employed as well as its first position. Beginning at four notes per beat, the metronome may be started at 60 and worked up gradually to 144, where alternate speeds of two and four notes per beat may be used. These exercises are given as the minimum amount needed.

Five-finger exercises, which Johnstone claims should not be taken indiscriminately at first, are valuable in developing ease and rapidity after the pupil has mastered the management of his fingers, and has trained his attention to control them fully. Of the many sets published, he considers Schmidt's "Daily Finger Exercises" ample for all ordinary requirements. But they should be played with constant mental care, and taken through all keys that offer any new black-and-white combinations. Johnstone states that he never had a pupil, no matter how advanced, who passed beyond being benefited by this collection, and when many ill-trained students, on coming to him, objected to such "beginners' work," he told them that their only hope of success lay in learning to play these exercises properly.

He advises the exercises numbered from 3 to 33 inclusive for the first and the chief work. Each one is to be repeated ten times, or even more, until the student feels that something has been gained. With a metronome (M. M.) of 60 to 72 at first, each may be taken twice with two notes to a beat, and then twice with four instead of two. When the exercise can be played at 96 with four notes to a beat, all tones being loud and equal, and all fingers properly lifted, he may proceed to the next exercise.

Four exercises are advised for each day's practice. They may be played each day in three major and three minor keys, taking a different group each day so that the schedule of keys is completed in every four days. Then for the two remaining days of each week six keys may be taken. Each exercise is to be repeated five times in each key at a metronome mark of 96, alternating two and four notes to each beat. Continue this method until the first hundred exercises are done, watching carefully to see that the finger-action is correct in rapid as well as slow *tempo*.

Another method is then suggested. Using one or two exercises for each day's work, play each exercise in all the twenty-four major and minor keys without stopping even when changing keys. Repeat the exercise three times, playing at first two notes, then three and four, to each beat. Begin with M. M. 96, and work up gradually to 184. Playing notes grouped in fours with an accent on every third note will be found difficult at first; but a constant watch on the accent will make it practicable, and will prove an excellent training in the mental control of rhythm. The changing accent will also help to equalize the power of the fingers. The Schmidt exercises from 3 to 33, and those in double notes from 119 on, will be found useful in this method. For the most part, the two hands are to be practised separately. This course, or one similar to it, will extend over five or six years; and no pupil should fail to go through at least some daily work of this sort. Among other useful collections, Johnstone mentions Mason's "Touch and Technique," part I; the Cotta-Lebert "Pianoforte School," part I; Germer's "Technique"; Raphael Joseffy's "Advanced Exercises"; and the Tausig-Ehrlich "Daily Studies," part I. All exercises are to be memorized, so that the hands may receive full attention. In an hour and a half of daily practice, at least fifteen minutes should be devoted to finger exercises, say five for each hand separately and five for the two hands together. Less than this is of little use, while much more will prove fatiguing. Thus for four hours a day, Pauer advises thirty minutes in the morning for exercises and scales, and twenty minutes in the afternoon for exercises. The time-tables suggested for practice are given at the end of this article.

Scale work may be safely delayed until the correct use of hand and fingers has become a well-established habit. In scale-playing, the hand is to be held rather high, which will aid the thumb movements and give a full stroke for the weak fourth and fifth fingers. The thumb must of course move toward its next key as soon as it has released any tone.

Johnstone gives the following suggestions:

1. Keep the hands as high above the keys as convenient.

2. Instead of holding the hands at right angles to the keys, let them lean outward a little, so that the fingers of one hand slope toward those of the other; and keep them at the same angle by continually moving the wrists along. In this way the thumb will reach its key more easily than otherwise. (The hand, however, must not lean outward toward the little finger. The outward bend of the wrist, as given in the Leschetizky method, merely brings the outer finger-tips farther away from the edge of the keys, giving the thumb more room to pass under the fingers.)

3. The joint of the thumb should be bent only slightly, so that the angular position of the wrist will let the outer part of the thumb lie straight along the key. When the correct bend is once found, it should not be changed, and all sidewise movement is to be accomplished from the root-joint. The movement from one thumb note to the next should be a gradual progress, and not a spasmodic jerk at the last minute. Thus in the scale of C the thumb is moved from C to E while the second finger is on D, and from E to F while the third finger strikes E.

4. After the thumb strikes F, care must be taken to shift the fingers onward over it by a motion of the whole hand, so that the fingers may be kept in their proper position, and not twisted out of their correct angle by any sudden jerk. "The correct action," according to Johnstone, "is to move the whole hand on, keeping it all the time at the same angle with the keys, and while moving it on, to lift it up again high above the keys to its original position." This would seem to imply that the playing of the thumb brings the hand down, which is hardly advisable. The hand may be held fairly high, but too much height, necessitating any great drop in playing with the thumb, should be avoided.

5. Any movement that puts any finger into a wrong position for striking is a wrong movement. Under this head come excessive bending of the thumb, straightening the fingers too much, curving them too much, etc.

6. These directions apply even more strongly in *arpeggio* playing, where the skips are wider and the difficulties consequently greater. The wrist movement, however, must never be so rapid as to tend to drag the fingers off the keys.

7. The wrist should not be dropped for a thumb note. (It would seem from rule 4, however, that the hand may be swung down a little, while keeping the height of the wrist unchanged. Such a swing, however, must be made as small as possible.)

8. Fingers should not be dropped to grope for the note before striking, nor should they delay in releasing their notes. Thumb notes must not be too loud, nor fourth-finger notes too weak.

9. In all scale and *arpeggio* practice, the work should be begun in slow *tempo,* with fingers acting rapidly when their turn comes. Such slow practice is not alone necessary for the beginner, but should be kept up by the advanced student, in alternation with rapid work. Its omission will increase the chance for inaccuracy.

10. A year of earnest study should be enough to familiarize the pupil with the major scales; but whatever time is required, he should never be allowed to go farther until he is sure of the right method and the correct fingering for each scale practised. The fourth finger should receive special attention, as, if this one works correctly the others will be fairly sure to do so too. Six months should then prove enough for the harmonic minor scales, and six more for the melodic minors.

11. Each scale should be repeated without pause, some ten to twenty times, through a compass of four or five octaves. For the first six months, the two hands should be taken separately; after that, they may be used together for part of the time.

Since scale passages often occur in varying rhythms, Johnstone advocates the use of a metronome, and the playing of many rhythmic figures, such as an eighth-note followed by two sixteenths, an eighth followed by a triplet of sixteenths, and so on. The chromatic scale is of course to be included in the general practice. Scales in thirds, sixths, and tenths must be taken up, as well as in octaves. Both parallel and contrary motion should be used. Scales should be practised starting from the top as well as from the bottom. The student will find it practicable to work on certain scales and *arpeggios* one week, and a new set during the next week. Dr. Harding's "5,000 Scale and Arpeggio Tests," and Johnstone's "Royal Method for Scales and Arpeggios," are both recommended. As the student gains in ease and power, he may gradually increase the speed until he can play eight notes to a beat at M. M. 96; but he must never forget to include slow and consciously accurate practice with each day's work.

The scales are to be played at all degrees of power, from the softest to the loudest; and also with variations of power in a single scale, as well as *staccato.* A soft and even scale may be obtained with relaxed muscles, but should not be attempted until the forcible scale from well-lifted fingers has been fully mastered. For technical endurance, Johnstone advises the "Scale of Scales," given by Mme. Brée in the Leschetizky method, in this volume. Ambitious students are advised to attempt scales in double thirds and sixths. At least fifteen minutes of daily practice on scales is needed to insure any real progress, while much more time may be given to this matter with profit.

Broken chords are emphasized as being a good preparation for *arpeggios.* The exercises for the former are arranged in four grades, each to be studied from six to twelve months, according to the pupil's ability. The first grade contains broken common chords in various figures and inversions, for a fixed position of the hand. The second grade consists of these figures arranged in succession and altered so that the hand may move gradually up or down the keyboard. Grade three takes up dominant and diminished seventh-chord figures, in all inversions, for fixed positions; while the fourth grade takes these in figures that ascend or descend successively. Each of the exercises in this group should be practised in every key, major and minor. Each should be repeated from ten to twenty times, with the metronome. The exercises are to be taken with each hand separately at first, and slowly, the speed being doubled and quadrupled later on. In those with fixed positions, the thumb and little finger may be held over notes an octave apart, when practicable, and the other fingers over their proper notes. Germer, Cotta-Lebert, and Mason give such exercises, while Johnstone has published a manual of them.

After a year or so of broken-chord exercises, *arpeggios* may be taken up. They should be studied in definite order, according to their varying difficulty. First come major common-chord *arpeggios*, separate hands, in the first position only. Second, minor common-chord *arpeggios*. Third, both of these groups with both hands together. Fourth, the second and third positions of these chords, with each hand singly at first, then both together. Fifth, *arpeggios* on the dominant and diminished sevenths, with separate hands, in all inversions. Sixth, the same with both hands together. Seventh, all the chords previously taken, in parallel motion, in sixths and tenths. Johnstone gives tables of fingering, but this may be studied from the section treating of it in the Leschetizky method, in this volume.

The faults of scale-playing are apt to be emphasized in *arpeggios*. The thumb should move onward quickly and evenly. The wrists should be bent outward. The hands should be held high, avoiding any sagging of the little-finger side. The whole hand should be kept raised as it passes the thumb. An even, onward movement of the hand, with little or no change in the angle it makes with the keyboard, is what is wanted. Care must be taken not to break the *legato* by a too early release of the note played just before the thumb strikes on passing under. It is a good idea to repeat each *arpeggio* until it has been played correctly three times in succession, with the metronome at any convenient speed. Various rhythms and tone-qualities may be used. At first the *arpeggio* may be practised through two octaves, but it should be extended afterward to four or five. Slow and rapid practice may be alternated. Johnstone advises fifteen minutes a day as a minimum for the beginner, and half an hour for the average pupil. For exercises to cultivate endurance, he recommends the "Scale of Arpeggios" and "Suite of Arpeggios" by Mme. Brée, given in this volume with the Leschetizky method.

Wrist and arm technique are covered by special exercises. Suppleness and accuracy are the points to aim for at first, with speed of action coming gradually. The following details are to be observed.

1. Raise the hand rapidly till it is nearly at right angles with the arm, keeping the proper curve of the fingers unaltered; hold the hand thus uplifted for some seconds; then swing it down to strike the note as rapidly as possible. A single note may be repeated. The succession of notes may be slow, but the actual up-and-down motions must be rapid.

2. Hold the wrist fairly low, nearly on a level with the keyboard.

3. Keep the forearm steady, and the arm muscles as relaxed as possible. The elbow moves only slightly, the wrist being the pivot.

4. Keep the fingers always properly curved, and do not let the hand waver before it descends to strike.

The single note may be practised with the middle finger at first, and the other fingers afterward. Then there may come repetitions of thirds, sixths, major triads, minor triads, dominant sevenths, and diminished sevenths. Begin slowly, say with M. M. 60 and one note to a beat. It is never wise to tire the wrist and arm muscles, so these exercises may be taken for a few minutes at a time, several times a day. Merely shaking the hand up and down in the air will prove useful.

The following are arranged for beginners, so that wrist development may keep abreast of finger training.

1. With the middle finger, strike each note of the scale ten times in succession, with wrist action, at M. M. 60. Repeat, twice as fast.

2. When some weeks have brought about increased power and flexibility, double the speed again, playing four notes to a beat at M. M. 60. The hand cannot be raised so high for such rapid work, but the slow practice must be kept up for part of the time. The hands may be practised separately for a year.

3. With the various fingers, as before, double the speed again. Then try *staccato* scales.

4. After some time on the single notes, use major and minor thirds and sixths.

5. Practise wrist action with the major triads on each note of the chromatic scale. Do this first with two chords to the beat, then four, then a succession of ascending and descending chords. It is advisable to introduce here the various rhythmic figures used for scales.

6. Apply the wrist action to the minor common chords and the dominant and diminished sevenths chords, in all inversions.

The stretch between little finger and thumb must always be kept fairly large. Finally the chords may be practised as octave *arpeggios*.

Four-note chords with the octave added to the triad may be played with repetitions, on all scale degrees. Five-note chords, consisting of seventh chords with the octave added, may also be used. A chord may then be played upward and downward through all its inversions. For purposes of power, the arm may be used to reinforce the wrist. The striking of chords by the upward throw of the wrist is advocated also. For octave work, Johnstone recommends Leybach's "La Diabolique," book IV of Mason's "Touch and Technique," Kullak's "Octave School," and his own "Royal Road to Octave and Wrist Technique." After mastering a fair amount of exercises, it is enough if these are used in practice, and new passages taken only as they occur in new pieces.

Among daily studies, in their order of progressive difficulty, Johnstone recommends the following:

1. Plaidy, "Daily Studies."
2. Loeschhorn, "Technical Studies."
3. Leybach, "La Diabolique" (a single wrist study).
4. Köhler, "Technische Materialen."
5. Germer, "Technics of the Piano."
6. Czerny, "Forty Daily Exercises," op. 337.
7. Hanon, "Le Pianiste Virtuose."
8. Moore, "The Mechanism of Pianoforte-Playing."
9. Mason, "Touch and Technique" (four books).
10. Kullak, "Octave School," books II and III.
11. Beringer, "Daily Studies."
12. Joseffy, "School of Advanced Piano-Playing."
13. Tausig-Ehrlich, "Daily Studies," three books.

Johnstone thinks that with such an elaborate course of exercises as has been outlined, piano studies, or Études, are hardly necessary. He believes that with the amount of time spent on technique, the rest of the time would be best devoted to good music. Études exist in large numbers, composed by the greatest geniuses and played by the most eminent performers. These works, though, were written before the recent systems of finger technique were fully evolved. The Étude is valuable as a "sugar-coated pill," however, as by its use the student thinks he is playing a piece while he is really doing technical work also. But the works of Czerny, Clementi, Moscheles, Henselt, Chopin, and all the others who composed Études, have certainly been a valuable legacy, in spite of any one's ideas to the contrary. Johnstone himself gives a graded list of such pieces, which will be found at the end of this article.

———

Before various points are brought up for discussion, another method will be described here, which differs radically from that of Johnstone in many points. This is the Deppe method, as given by Ehrenfechter and as altered later by Breithaupt into his own method.

The position at the piano is lower in the Deppe method than in others. Deppe said, "You may have the soul of an angel, but if you sit high, the tone will not be poetic." If one sits high, the arm, hand, and fingers form nearly a straight line, and the weight of the arm bears too much upon the wrist and fingers. If one sits low, with the elbow one or two inches below the level of the keyboard, then the arm will assume its proper shape. There will thus be no leaning or pressing of the arm on the hand. The arm is well bent at both the elbow and the wrist, and the muscles are ready

for action and amenable to the effect of practice. Bodily movements are to be avoided, except, of course, a leaning to one side or the other as demanded by the location of the notes.

The arm has to sustain the hand and guide its movements, requiring for this both strength and mobility. A simple exercise for strengthening the arm consists of holding the fingers on the keys without pressing them down, and maintaining this position until tiredness begins to set in. After a rest, this may be done again, and the whole repeated several times a day. This can be done at a table, or simply in the air. Arm strength and weight is the basis of this method, as indicated by Deppe's remark, "The arm should be like lead, the wrist like a feather." Another exercise consists of putting the fingers on the key-surfaces, as before, moving the arms out gradually until the hands reach the ends of the keyboard, and then bringing them gradually back to the centre again. The beauty of this exercise, according to Ehrenfechter, lies in the fact that it can be practised without disturbing the neighbors.

The wrist must be held high. The actual height will differ in individual cases, but it should always be fairly great, to bring the muscles into a state of tension. A high wrist makes practice more fatiguing, but there will be a corresponding gain in quick and safe attainment of desired results. Yet great care must be taken to avoid any stiffening of the wrist, as flexibility is of the utmost importance. To keep the wrist flexible, hold it high, but free from all constraint. When any one complains of a weak wrist, it is probably the arm that is weak. As an illustration, the lion's paw is suggested. This seems flabby in appearance, but contains an immense amount of strength. As not every one can keep a lion for scientific purposes, ordinary elastic is also mentioned as an example of force without rigidity.

The back of the hand should be on a line with the keyboard, which evidently means that it should be level. The side nearest the little finger may even be elevated a trifle, or at least held consciously high, so as to give more scope for the fourth and fifth finger, and to strengthen that side of the hand as a whole. This action, however, should not be allowed to draw the elbow away from the side. The hand does not move of itself in playing, but is made to glide along as a whole by the arm. The raising of the hand from the wrist is rated as a false action.

The fingers, according to this method, are blamed for many things that are not really their fault. Their duty is merely to touch the keys in slow or quick succession, under simple or complex conditions. Too often, instead of being guided by the arm, they are forced to support it, and drag it from one position to the other. With the duties of the arm and wrist properly performed, the fingers are free to do their own work, and can do it with much less chance of error. Ehrenfechter sums up with the following rule: "Let the arm sustain the hand in its proper position, carry, conduct its movements and with it bring every finger right upon the key which it is intended to touch."

The fingers must be trained for flexibility and independence. Some hands are more adapted than others to this end, but the best hand needs training, and even the worst will be benefited by it. Mere strength is not the end in view, although it comes with practice; but mobility and agility are what is needed. The fourth finger is strong enough in proportion when compared with the others, but owing to the position of certain muscular bands it is comparatively lacking in flexibility. Stiff fingers, which often come from stiff wrists, may be avoided by training the muscles of the arm, hand, and fingers as one large system.

The touch, or method of striking the keys with the fingers, is held to be more of a pressure than a blow, and similar to the organ touch. The fact that the fingers assume a hammer-shape, it is here claimed, has misled many into making them strike like a hammer. The Deppe method asserts that there is no need for a long finger-stroke from a high position, that it does not improve the quality of tone, that it prevents fulness in soft passages, and that it places too great a strain on the finger muscles.

By instinct and experiment, Liszt came to play in the way directed by Deppe, the latter actually taking some of his methods from Liszt's example. Amy Fay, in her book "Music Study in Germany," speaks of this matter thus: "After Deppe had directed my attention to it, I remembered I had never seen Liszt lift up his fingers so fearfully high as the other schools, and especially the Stuttgart one, made such a point of doing. . . . Liszt had such an extraordinary way of playing a melody. It did not seem to be so loud and cut out as most artists make it, and yet it was so penetrating." Of his touch, she said, "The notes seemed just to ripple off his finger ends with scarce any perceptible motion." Deppe reasoned from Liszt's example that the secret consisted of playing with the weight instead of striking a blow. The fingers sink down with the key, but do not put forth any great muscular exertion.

The tone produced by this method will be very weak at first, but will gain constantly in power, sonority, and brilliance. This tone is not beaten out of the piano, but with increased sensitiveness of the finger-tips will appear to be drawn from it. The beginner must keep strictly to this method of tone production, and if the tone seems too weak, he must not try to increase it by any false mechanism.

Deppe made his pupils listen to every tone, carry it into the next for a *legato,* and make sure that it had no more and no less prominence than every other tone. The fingers are kept well curved, so that the notes are played by the tips. The fingers, however, are not spread out over their notes, but kept close together, though without any constraint. In playing the first five notes of the scale of C, for example, the right arm will move a trifle to the right before each

note is played by a finger, in order to bring that finger directly over its note. The same principle, of course, applies to the left hand. As a rule, the thumb is very slightly bent, and its tip kept near that of the forefinger when it is not needed elsewhere. Slow practice is kept up for a long time. No distinction is made between a *legato* and *staccato* touch, the latter being the same as the former, but followed by a quick release of the tone.

The tension and contraction of the hand is brought about by the separating of the thumb from the other fingers, which are still held in a group, and by the return of the thumb and the finger-group toward each other. The greatest contraction, of course, takes place when the thumb and little finger come together on the same key.

In studying finger-exercises, slow speed, strict attention to *legato,* and perfect equality of tone are the three points to be observed. The use of rhythm, bringing accents on certain notes, is considered wrong. Exercises with one or more notes held down during practice are condemned on the ground that they afford an undesirable rest for the arm, which should be kept in action as a support for the hand. Any resting of the arm on held notes will tend to stiffen the wrist and prevent the free fall of the fingers. Hand-guides like those of Kalkbrenner or Bohrer are therefore to be put aside as dangerous. The use of mental concentration and attention while playing exercises is insisted upon, and is considered necessary for true progress, as well as an aid in making practice interesting instead of dry and dull. Miss Fay found such concentration very exhausting, and after two or three hours of it would feel ready to drop off her chair. All exercises should be practised in every key, thus making the fingers familiar with the black keys as well as the white ones, and preparing the way for scales.

In making long skips, for which the hand has not enough stretch, the fingers must still be carried by the arm without assuming a slanting position. The hand will therefore describe nearly a semicircle, rising to some height before moving sidewise, and coming down vertically at the last. In going from white to black keys, the finger must not be stretched out, but the proper curve maintained, and the necessary motion made by the arm.

In scale practice the mental concentration must be kept up to its fullest extent. The chief technical difficulty here is, of course, the management of the thumb, which must pass from one part of the scale to another. The gradual motion of the hand, according to Ehrenfechter, will bring the thumb nearly to the required position for F in the scale of C, and will practically do away with the need of underpassing. "All that is needed," says Ehrenfechter, "is for the middle finger to go politely out of the way in order to allow the thumb to pass on to its key." The same principle applies in coming down the scale. When the notes have been played downward from C to F, the hand has moved gradually toward the thumb to such an extent that the middle finger is comfortably near its E. This method of scale playing, it will be noticed, differs radically from the under-passed and prepared-touch method used by Leschetizky. The major scales in sharp keys, up to five sharps, are fingered like that of C. The flat scales, including G-flat, have various fingerings, because of the rule that the thumb is not to come on a black key; but Ehrenfechter thinks this rule a needless bit of archaic pedantry.

He recommends practising the scales in both parallel and contrary motion, and states that the latter is very important in developing the arm muscles. Thirds, sixths, and tenths, are also mentioned. The practising of scales in rhythmic figures, or with different and varying degrees of power, is not endorsed. The important point is considered to be the development of perfectly even tones. Rhythm and control of power are taught in connection with other music.

Arpeggios are, of course, considered valuable, and are to be prolonged through three or four octaves. Their influence in strengthening the arm and wrist, and giving the fingers independence, is very great. Of the many varieties, the chord of the seventh, both major and minor, is recommended as the best. Both parallel and contrary motion are to be used, and the different inversions as well as the first position.

Firm chords are still played with pressure rather than with a blow. In these, however, it is usually advisable to stiffen the wrist, so that the chord is aided by the force of the arm. The fingers will stiffen of their own accord, when they are stretched out to take their proper notes. When going from one chord to another, the hand may be allowed to relax after each chord has played, and rest on the keys.

With Ehrenfechter, the high raising of hand and arm is not a preparation for striking a chord, but another method of relaxation. In music of technical difficulty, this change of position will rest the arm, as keeping it in a single position is much more fatiguing. In coming down on a chord, however, it is not to be played from a height, but the hand is checked just above the keys, and the chord played with the usual method of pressure. When chords are some distance apart on the keyboard, the hand must rise vertically from one and descend vertically on the next; so it may describe the semicircle mentioned in connection with single-note skips.

In performing the *tremolo,* or repeated notes, the fingers must not be allowed to glide off the keys as if dusting them—a too frequent fault, according to Ehrenfechter. Each finger plays the note just as the preceding finger is releasing it. In order to bring the fingers into their proper position for this, the hand must move sidewise even more noticeably than when playing the scale. Liszt sometimes calls for repeated thirds, which may be given with alternating hands. In this case the fingers are held stiff, and in a more vertical position than usual, with the left hand under the right.

The trill requires a maximum of finger flexibility and independence. The tips of the two fingers used must never leave the keys, and must press them down to their full depth. The two tones must, of course, be kept even in power. The speed must be perfectly regular and even. Whatever speed is taken at the start must be maintained; but this should be as great as the performer can make it.

The use of the pedal for mere loudness or force of tone is discouraged as being inartistic. It is advised, however, in sustaining a bass part where skips prevent the left hand from holding the tones, as well as in its more general purpose of sustaining harmonies whenever desired. Liszt and Thalberg were masters of the pedal, and Amy Fay says of Liszt's playing: "The secrets are his touch and his peculiar use of the pedal; he has a way of disembodying a piece from the piano and seeming to make it float in the air. He makes a spiritual form of it so perfectly visible to your inward eye, that it seems as if you could almost hear it breathe! Deppe seems to have almost the same idea. . . . He played a few bars of a Sonata, and in his whole method of binding the notes together and managing the pedal I recognized Liszt. The thing floated! Unless Deppe wishes the chord to be very brilliant, he takes the pedal *after* the chord instead of simultaneously with it. This gives a very ideal sound."

The soft pedal is considered rather unnecessary by Ehrenfechter. He holds that a player should be capable of producing by his touch all the needed gradations of softness. According to him, "To the true artist of refined taste, the effect of the mutilated tone-quality produced cannot be otherwise than painful. True, in some exceptional cases composers have marked *una corda;* if the player uses it in such instances, he has then the excuse that he does not do so on his own responsibility."

Good fingering in piano playing is of the utmost importance. *Legato* work cannot be well done without it, and it is a great aid in training the hand and bringing about a good style of performance. This matter must be taken up in the early stages of study—one of the many reasons why it is advisable to have a good teacher even for beginners. A good fingering is one that is easy and does not interfere with expression. Many cases for special procedure will occur in actual study, but the following few rules will almost always prove useful:

1. Any passage that can be conveniently played without altering the position of the hand should be fingered on that basis.

2. When change of position is necessary, the fingering should be such as to cause the fewest possible changes.

3. Use the nearest finger to a key, unless there is some definite reason for doing otherwise.

In running passages the fingering for diatonic and chromatic scales and broken chords will generally suggest the proper fingering for use. Sometimes, in rapid work, it is permissible to pass one finger over another.

The fourth may be passed over the fifth, or the middle finger over either of its neighbors, when this will give a better result than the more usual procedure.

For polyphonic music, a good command of fingering is especially necessary. The "Twenty-Four Preludes and Fugues" of Bach, as fingered by Tausig, are recommended to the student. Other works mentioned as giving good examples of fingering are Clementi's "Gradus," fingered by Tausig, the Études of Chopin, and the works of Liszt. For the earlier pieces, the works of Clementi, Dussek, Steibelt, Kuhlau, and others of the sort will give a sufficient repertoire; while for the advanced student the great classical and modern composers' works offer an almost unlimited field. But the student should not forget that progress depends more upon the technical exercises than upon the pieces learned.

————————

According to Breithaupt (whose technique is described by himself in his "School" and in "The Musician," Vol. XVI, for 1911) Deppe was the first to make proper use of the upper arm and shoulder, but he "undid all the good by his unfortunate tension and stiffening of the joints (so-called fixation) and the turning in of the hands at a sharp angle." The weight idea was developed by Deppe's pupil Bandmann, with suggestions from Busoni, while Breithaupt himself was enlightened by the school and example of Carreño. The chief idea of the Breithaupt system is the avoidance of muscular tension as much as possible, and the playing by weight from the shoulder, elbow, wrist, or knuckle, as the case may be. Liszt's playing is cited as an example of the proper qualities, as follows:

1. Playing with complete relaxation of the muscles and joints.

2. Using to the fullest extent the massive weight of the whole arm and its parts, and playing from the shoulder.

3. Employing skilfully the various correct motions, such as the swing, the forearm roll, and the forearm extension.

4. Playing with loose "slung" fingers and easily dropping hand.

Opposed to the school of weight-playing is the school of finger-technique. But even the great players of the latter school make use of some of the motions advised in the former. Tone is always to be obtained by weight, combined with the fingers in the right way, and is not so well produced by fingers alone. Breithaupt enumerates the following "mechanical sources of tone-producing action."

1. The falling swing or "throw."

2. The balance of the mass.

3. The forearm roll and combined upper-arm roll.

4. The forearm extension and bending (erection of the hand and gliding function).

5. The *vibrato,* or vertical *tremolo* as distinguished from the roll or horizontal *tremolo.*

6. The loose throw of the long "swung" fingers.

In playing by weight with the whole arm or forearm, these swing down toward the keyboard, where they are stopped by the striking of the fingers. In this stopping, the knuckle joint takes whatever muscular effort is needed, the wrist being kept as loose as the playing will allow. When the note or notes have been struck, immediate relaxation should follow, the shoulder then taking the weight of the arm, and a loose wrist giving sufficient weight to keep the keys held down. The muscular tension is therefore only momentary, and should always be followed by the relaxation. With good players, this habit of relaxing becomes natural and unconscious. The same is true after the lighter tone given by the falling wrist.

No definite rule can be made for the position of the hand. With good instruction and faithful practice, each hand will find the positions in which it produces the best results with the least proportionate effort. The structure of the hand, the length of the fingers, and the width of the stretch, are all factors. In general, small and solid hands will take a high position with curved fingers, while long and narrow hands will adapt themselves to the flat position with extended fingers and low wrist. But in transmitting the weight of a swing, the knuckle should usually be well bent.

The movements of the hand may be a vertical swing, a partial rotation or roll, and a turning inward or outward when needed. The swing is used with single tones, ordinary chords, octaves, and so on. The rotary movement is applicable for trills, broken chords, and any progressions that need a side-to-side motion of the hand. The outward and inward turnings are more infrequent, being used at the ends of scales and passages or if the thumb must reach in to a black key.

The vertical swing from the wrist is more noticeable in slow *tempo* than in rapid work. As it grows less in the latter, it gradually becomes a delicate vibration, suitable and desirable for octave work. The wrist must always seem light and flexible. The forcible bending back of the hand and a stroke with muscular tension must be avoided. The forearm extension, or pushing the arm toward the hand so that the wrist is raised over the fingers, is also of use in octave playing.

The thumb and its extension in the hand must absolutely be kept relaxed at all times. The hand turns with the arm, and the fingers give way, releasing a tone to allow for underpassing or overpassing. The thumb must never be held stiffly underneath the palm, as that will contract the hand and limit freedom of movement. The thumb should turn with the arm, and at the proper time be loosely thrown under the hand to its key. It should not grasp the key spasmodically, but should drop on it naturally. This can be done without interfering greatly with the *legato.*

The rotary motion may become quite noticeable in finishing a scale or *arpeggio,* the hand coming off the keyboard with its palm visible.

When a scale does not end at its outer limit, but starts back toward the centre of the keyboard, the finishing roll is not very great, and is reversed at the turn with an easy swing that is made by the whole arm.

Finger movements are right if they combine with the natural swing of the relaxed arm, or if they are done with the most ease and the least effort. The usual idea of developing muscle-energy in the fingers is called false by Breithaupt. This is not saying that finger-dexterity is useless, but that it should be cultivated as a part of the arm-system. The finger movements are swinging movements from a loosely sustained arm and hand, and demand no great muscular exertion. The finger swings from the knuckle, and as it strikes the key down, the weight of the arm and hand is allowed to rest upon it for an instant. The usual relaxation and "discharge of weight from the key" must follow at once. The relaxation must be so complete that the fingers could be easily knocked off the keys, say by the other hand. In the finger-throw, it is a matter of personal choice whether the hand is held high, medium, or flat.

If the finger-swing is limited so that the weight of the finger alone brings its tip on the key, then a very light tone results, which is useful in rapid passages of soft character. In this lightest and most refined form of touch, each finger works by itself, and the relaxation should give an independence so perfect that each one can fall by itself, and not add to the weight of the others. When this result is attained, the way is clear to develop the greatest speed and dexterity. This light finger-action must be only momentary, and any little muscular impulse that is given to aid the drop must be followed by the usual instantaneous relaxation.

The old method of overexerting the finger muscles, it is claimed, stiffened the finger in the knuckle; overstrained the muscles by a too extreme lift; kept up the tension without relaxing after the stroke; and sometimes even called for an extra afterpressure. These points are all regarded as errors, since they tend to increase fatigue.

In the Breithaupt system, then, which is taught also by Steinhausen and others, there is no attempt to use absolute finger-power. The attack is produced largely or wholly by falling weight, even when fingers only are used. The question of when muscular tension shall be added (always with the weight of the loose arm back of it in greater or less degree) is one that depends on practical experience and the needs of musical expression. It is stated, however, that from 60 to 80 per cent. of finger-attack should be used with nothing more than the falling hand-weight. The *non-legato* is the usual style, with a large amount of *legato* roll, in which the fingers are lifted very slightly and with little muscular tension. The weight determines the effect. *Staccato,* too, is not to be played by a muscular raising of the finger after the stroke, but by lifting it off the key. It is claimed that playing as a whole will average 40 per cent. *non-legato* with hand-fall, 30 per cent. *legato* with arm-rolling, 10 per cent. *staccato* with vibrating hand, 10 per cent. octaves and repeated chords, and the remaining 10 per cent. with more or less active power in the finger-muscles.

Weight-playing is claimed to be correct, then, because it saves fatigue. It differs from the older school in the following points:

It develops the whole arm instead of merely the finger and hand.

Just as clock-hands are moved by a spring, so the finger action depends on the arm action.

The elbow is kept flexible instead of stiff.

The arm and shoulder also are kept flexible.

The fingers are thrown loosely instead of forced down stiffly.

All joints are kept relaxed as much as possible, instead of stiff.

The keys are pressed by a fall of weight instead of beaten down.

In general, weight is used instead of muscular tension.

The training is begun from the shoulder instead of the fingers.

The whole principle is summed up again by Breithaupt thus:

"We must let the playing members hang, let them 'go'; all the muscles must be loose. We balance the weight and preserve the relaxed condition in all motions and positions, excepting those where, for æsthetic reasons, the opposite condition, firmness, is especially required."

———————

In looking over these methods, we find that there are three main ideas or systems. The principles given by Johnstone sum up a fairly widespread set of teaching methods. Leschetizky altered these by certain clever devices for the use of the fingers. Breithaupt, going beyond the Deppe method, opposes the great exertion of the finger-muscles, and substitutes playing largely or wholly by weight. Certainly there is choice enough here to satisfy any one, or to justify almost any teacher in his procedure. It is none too easy to decide which is correct, or to be sure that any single method is wholly correct and the others all wrong. Johnstone says of the relaxing system, and the gentle lifting up and down of the fingers, "This plan is no doubt exceedingly simple and exceedingly easy; but by its fruits it must be condemned. Is this not the very style and method of every unregenerate son of Adam when he comes to his first lesson with a bunch of feeble fingers all moving together if one is moved? . . . Simplicity is useless if it is ineffective. Whether are power, control, and independence to be gained by allowing our hand muscles to remain in their normal condition of weakness, flabbiness, and interdependence, and by feebly raising and dropping each finger; or by practising a strong, high uplift of each finger and a forcible downstroke; at the same time holding the other fingers motionless, so as to isolate each and detach it from the influence of the others as much as possible? The very statement of the conflicting views is a sufficient answer to the whole question." But apart from any unclearness in the involved interrogation, Johnstone speaks as if the Breithaupt school did not strive for independence of fingers, which it certainly mentions as necessary.

If we are to judge them by their fruits, then nearly all methods have produced great pianists. That, however, is not entirely the point. The real issue is whether any one pianist would achieve most by one or another method. This cannot be answered by experiment, as one man can learn but one method at a time; and it is hardly possible to find students so equal in ability that one of such a group could be started in each method, for purposes of comparison. A better idea of the relative merits may be obtained by taking a number of single points in them for discussion or contrast.

The first point is the very important question of whether muscle-playing or weight-playing is correct. The latter is undoubtedly used, in part at least, by every great artist, and often with a low wrist. It is possible, however, for the pianist to get his education in the muscle-method, and then perform by the weight-method. The tremendous tone of a Paderewski will show that this is probably the case with him; for he was a Leschetizky pupil, and must have developed his fingers and their muscles in his course of study.

The question then arises, would muscular finger-training interfere in any way with later weight-playing? The answer would seem to be a decided negative. However strong the hand and fingers may become, there should never be any difficulty in relaxing them. However firmly the arm, shoulder, and elbow may be held, there is never any trouble about making their muscular exertion cease. The ease of relaxation is so great that long habits of firmness will not prevent the utmost laxity of muscles whenever it is desired. It would seem, then, that the acquiring of finger dexterity and control could be done by the Leschetizky method, even if such control were used afterward in the weight system. The Breithaupt method may be the one that Liszt and other great pianists used in playing, but it is a fair question whether they did not arrive at this method through the muscular practice of finger exercises in their earlier days. In other words, while the Breithaupt method is proper and excellent in performance, it is possible that the student who starts in it and keeps to it wholly may not do quite as well as the student of another method, who acquired finger strength by definite training for it before changing to the weight-method in later times. A few more years should answer this, and give the pupils of the new system a chance to develop their powers and show results. Meanwhile it is certain that the Breithaupt method does give strength to the fingers through the exercise they get in holding up the arm-weight before

relaxation. It is also true of gymnastics in general that fairly light, regular exercise gives better results than violent straining. For real development, one does not have to exert himself to his utmost, until he drops from fatigue. This would show that extreme stretches and finger uplifts of the type advocated by Johnstone should not be encouraged.

The question of the prepared touch taught by Leschetizky is another point that will bear examining. Its effect on quality of tone is not an essential advantage, for the other methods train the students to a thorough control of dynamics. It is undoubtedly more useful as an aid to accuracy. The pianist who uses it is all the time making a conscious effort to place his fingers over the right notes, even while he is playing others that may be noticeably earlier in time. Yet it might cause awkwardness if carried to extremes, and should never be used in a passage that can be more easily played without it.

Scale practice is always an important part of the student's technical work. Leschetizky uses the prepared touch in this; but if the object of that touch is accuracy, then it is hardly so entirely necessary here. As far as accuracy is concerned, the notes of a scale come in an ordered succession that presents no difficulties to the mind of the player. Deppe's idea that the bunched hand should move along gradually and thus substitute a sidewise motion for underpassing is not very practical, and makes the smooth joining of the scale-parts rather uncertain, at least for the beginner. Breithaupt's throwing-under of the thumb is more feasible, but even so the thumb works better when the throw is aided by some muscular tension. The happy medium would seem to be a muscular under-passing of the thumb that falls just short of preparing it on its note while the third or fourth finger is holding the preceding note. This makes the thumb reach its position on time with less effort than if it is prepared after underpassing, and with about the same accuracy. But even if much preparing seems not fully necessary in scale work, it certainly does no harm; and it helps in the shifting along of the hand after the thumb plays its note, though here the preparation of the second finger alone would seem sufficient to guide the hand.

In large chords, the weight method would seem to have a decided advantage, even at the start.

The Leschetizky method is world-famous to-day, and has produced many pianists of the first rank. By this test it would seem to be good. But since it is so easy to adopt some of the Breithaupt procedure after learning the Leschetizky method, and since so many great pianists seem to do this, it is possible that the next great school will be a fusion of these two methods in teaching, keeping most of Leschetizky's ideas and adding enough of Breithaupt's to let the student who has mastered the former adopt the latter consciously instead of unconsciously. Certainly it would seem that it is better to have strong fingers, even if their full strength is not exerted in performances. As for the Breithaupt method, it stands to reason that if a single note is made to demand a smaller effort, more notes can be played with the same exertion previously used, and at a greater speed.

The teaching of interpretation is a more elastic matter, and one in which the different methods are practically in agreement. For purposes of reference, Johnstone enumerates the following works, among others.

Kullak, "Æsthetics of Pianoforte Playing."
Taylor, "Technique and Expression."
Kullak, "Beethoven's Piano Playing."
Marx, "Beethoven's Pianoforte Works."
Reinecke, "Letters on Beethoven's Sonatas."
Goodrich, "Theory of Interpretation."
Riemann, "Catechism of Pianoforte Playing."
Christiani, "Pianoforte Æsthetics."
Dannreuther, "Musical Ornamentation."
Weitzmann, "History of Pianoforte Playing."
Parry, "The Art of Music."
Hanslick, "The Beautiful in Music."
Johnstone, "Touch, Phrasing, and Interpretation."
Johnstone, "Phrasing in Piano-Playing, with Examples."
Johnstone, "The Art of Teaching Pianoforte Playing."

With these and other works on the subject, it is well covered. But the best guide is, of course, a good teacher. Failing that, those students who are forced to work by themselves after a limited amount of instruction will do well to hear great artists whenever possible, and notice carefully their phrasing, shading, and so on.

Some rules for melody-playing will be found in the translation of the Leschetizky method given in this volume, as well as a section on dynamics and shading. These condensed bits of advice will form a valuable guide for the beginner. There are also a number of suggestions which good taste can offer. In playing any piece, very few passages are to be taken at an absolute dead level of uniform force. There should always be little *nuances* of power, the amount and prominence of which will depend on the character of the piece. Notes within a measure are not always meant to be arbitrarily exact, and some of the time may often be given to certain notes at the expense of others. This does not usually extend beyond a single bar, but it may even do that in expressive short phrases. Such *tempo rubato* is most in place in works of strong emotional expression, such as those of Chopin. Phrasing depends largely on form, and the article on form in this volume will give the student a systematic grasp of the subject that is better than any "rule-of-thumb" procedure. For the smaller divisions in phrasing, which do not depend so definitely on musical form, there is still some guidance to be found in the length and structure of theme, antecedent, consequent, and other divisions; while if this is not apparent, common sense and good musical taste must come to the rescue. In polyphonic music, a unified *legato* and a melodic style for each part is desirable, with less abrupt transitions in shading, but some accent at the beginning and ending of the figures, to show their presence and limits to the listener.

For all these points, however, technical perfection is a necessity. The performer will be able to devote his whole attention to the phrasing, shading, and interpretation only when the technical difficulties of a piece are so fully mastered that they need little or no conscious mental attention. Then, and then only, will he be able to reach the highest flights of art, and show the best that is in him.

It seems wise to include here [. . .] a graded list of studies, which will be found of value by teachers as well as students.

LISTS OF GRADED STUDIES.

GRADE I.
Very Easy Studies for Elementary Pupils.

Berens, Opp. 70, 61, 73, 79.
Czerny, Opp. 353, 684, 139, 453.
Le Couppy, Op. 17.
Köhler, Opp. 151, 190, 205.
Wohlfahrt, Op. 61.

Duvernoy, Opp. 176, 110.
Döring, Opp. 38, 86.
Lemoine, Op. 37.
Loeschhorn, Opp. 159, 192.

GRADE II.
Easy Studies for Young Pupils.

Czerny, Op. 139.
Kirchner, Op. 71.
Köhler, Opp. 182, 216, 234.
Duvernoy, Op. 176.
Bergmüller, Op. 100.
Löschhorn, Opp. 65, 190, 193.
Germer, 100 Elementary Studies (Bosworth).

Gurlitt, Opp. 50, 51, 52, 53.
Kunz, Op. 14.
Döring, Op. 8.
Bertini, Op. 100.
Berens, Op. 73.
Le Couppey, Op. 79.
Bach, Small Preludes.

GRADE III.
Moderately Difficult Studies for Junior and Intermediate Pupils.

Bertini, Opp. 29 and 32.
Heller, Opp. 47, 45, 46.
Krause, Opp. 2, 9.
Hiller, Op. 46.
Löschhorn, Op. 66.
Berens, Op. 73.

Concone, Opp. 44, 24, 25, 30, 31.
Bach, Two-Part Inventions.
Bach, Suites.
Wolff, Opp. 261, 19.

Cramer's Studies, Ed. by Coccius, Bülow, Tausig, Ruthardt, or Dr. Weekes.

GRADE IV.
Studies for Senior Pupils.

Clementi, Gradus.
Czerny, Opp. 355, 740, 818, 553, 834.
Mäyer, Opp. 200, 119, 168, 305.
Löschhorn, Opp. 67, 136.
Heller, Op. 16.

Moscheles, Opp. 70 and 95.
Berens, Opp. 61, 64.
Berger, Opp. 12, 22.
Döring, Op. 8.
Köhler, Opp. 128, 138, 112.
Kessler, Op. 20.
Jensen, Opp. 32, 33.

GRADE V.
Studies for Advanced Students.

Alkan, Opp. 38, 39.
Köhler, Op. 120.
Nicodé, Op. 21.
Chopin, Opp. 10, 25.
Schumann, Opp. 3, 7, 10, 13.
MacDowell, Op. 46.
Brahms, 51 Technical Exercises.
Liszt, Concert Studies and Paganini Studies.
Bülow, Major, Minor and Chromatic Studies.

Rosenthal and Schytte, Pianoforte Virtuosity.
Pauer, New Gradus ad Parnassum.
Henselt, Opp. 2, 5.
Czerny, Opp. 335, 365, 735.
Thalberg, Op. 26.
Ravina, Op. 14.
Saint-Saëns, Op. 52.
Tausig, 12 Concert Studies.
Rubinstein, Concert Studies.

PRACTICAL HINTS ON PIANO STUDY

By IGNACE J. PADEREWSKI

[This article by the great pianist was very carefully prepared. It was told by him to an interviewer, who transferred the thoughts to paper. Then M. Paderewski went carefully over the manuscript. The article may, therefore, be said to represent M. Paderewski's exact views on piano-playing, prepared under the most careful conditions.]

THE first requisite to becoming a really good pianist is talent. I will say this, however: that, given good tuition, any one with the ability to work, and application to it, can learn to play; but it will not be artistic. Nearly every one has talent for something, and the great point is to discover that talent, to give it a fair trial in cultivation, and to stick to its development. If your talent is not for music, then find out in what branch it lies. Money—and time, which is still more precious, as it can never be regained—will be saved, the whole life turned into another channel, and its usefulness will be greatly increased.

But lack of energy or inclination for hard work must not be confounded with lack of talent. There are many with talent who are too lazy to work; such would not make a success in any art, no matter how great their aptitude. For this there is no excuse; any one can develop energy.

The first quality for the piano student is a natural musical gift, and then for its cultivation the energy for hard work, and the important requirement of a good, thorough teacher. In this last the responsibility of a choice rests with parents whose indifference or lack of insight may wreck the best prospects.

The sane, healthy way to study the piano is to apply one's thought directly to the work, laid out methodically by the teacher, for a certain length of time every day. That length of time depends entirely upon the future that the student may decide upon. If he or she takes up music as a professional, four hours daily should be given to study; if as an amateur, two hours is enough. In both cases the divisions of time devoted to practice should be not less than one hour.

The fault most general, not only with girl students but with professionals, is the sitting at the piano as a pastime instead of working seriously. There is no instrument that offers such inducement to idle away time as the piano. Instead of taking the study of it as a very earnest one, many fall into the way of looking upon it as an amusement, idling away hours in passing agreeably from one thing to another. These misspent hours end in a smattering of knowledge and a certain amount of faulty fluency, of no solid use when it comes to practical application.

Of course, in playing the piano the fundamental factor is technique, but that word technique includes everything. It includes not dexterity alone, as many mistakenly think, but also touch, rhythmic precision, and pedaling. That combination is what I call technical equipment.

I consider it my duty to say why I mean that true technique comprises everything. There are good artists who have only one or two of those factors of it that I have named. They may have good facility and strength, but no rhythm, and no knowledge of how to use the pedals. In this class it would be easy to find many great artists whose incomplete command of all that goes to make technique would confirm what I have said. Again, some have all but the beautiful tone. The true technique is not made up of one or more of its necessary factors, but it must comprise them all, and each demands its special training and study: dexterity, rhythm, correct pedaling, and tone.

In speaking, then, on the subject of piano-playing, what should first be considered are these very factors of technique and how to get them.

The length of time to be devoted daily to finger dexterity depends upon what stage of technical development the student is in. For those who have the fingers already prepared, naturally less time is required, and more may be given to the study of pieces. But, no matter what stage of progress the student has reached, one hour daily of this branch of technique is indispensable.

First, begin your study each day with the five-finger exercises and the scales. Play them slowly, very legato, and with a deep touch, giving particular attention in the scales to the passing of the thumb under the hand and of the hand over the thumb. The real secret of playing rapid, brilliant scales is this quick, quiet passing of thumb and hand, and by it many difficulties may be avoided.

The position of the hand in this is of great importance. In playing up the scale with the right hand, and in playing down the scale with the left, the part of the hand toward the thumb should be held considerably higher than the part toward the little finger. Thus, by raising the inner part of the hand next to the thumb, and dropping the outer part next to the little finger, there is more room for the thumb to pass under the fingers unobstructed and easily.

In coming down the scale with the right hand, and in going up with the left, the position of the hand should be reversed—that is, hold the hand lower toward the thumb, and higher toward the little finger. By observing this position you will already be partially prepared for the passing of the fingers over the thumb, and have also, as in the case of the first position mentioned, a shorter distance to go to strike the keys.

These positions of the hand are of utmost importance not only in scales, but also in acquiring fluency in arpeggios, and in passage-playing of all kinds.

With many the quality of tone is inborn, and connected with a natural sense of musical beauty. This depends, too, in great measure upon the construction of the hand and fingers. People with thick fingers have a natural tone, and consequently little difficulty in developing a beautiful touch. Others will have to work a great deal under good direction before they acquire that same beautiful tone. In the latter case the practising of slow passages with a deep touch, and without lifting the fingers very high, is most important. At the same time each separate tone should be listened to and its quality noted. The position of the hand in training depends on its natural construction, and requires individual treatment. For instance, in training, the strong hand with the thick fingers may be held even, with the knuckles down, while the weak hand with long fingers should be held with the back ball-shaped or arched, with the knuckles up.

In the training of the hand a great fault is very common, not only among amateurs, but even among professionals, and that is the bending out of the first joints of the fingers where their cushions touch the key. Such a position of the finger, its joint bent out, makes the getting of a good tone impossible. Students and teachers should pay great attention to the "breaking down" of the last joints of the fingers; it is a difficulty that must be settled in the very beginning. I even go so far as to say that those whose finger-joints "break down" should not play the piano unless they have energy enough to correct the fault, and it can be corrected.

The ability of producing a legato may be acquired by two means: First by careful fingering, and second, by the use of the pedal. In the first case the quick, careful passing of the thumb under the fingers is the practical factor, always studying slowly, with a deep touch, and listening closely to the binding together of the notes. In the second case the judicious use of the pedal is the aim.

As a hint to amateurs, I would say that it is a mistake to be afraid to use the pedal in playing scales. In quick scales the pedal may be most effectively used to give brilliance and color, but only under a certain rule. Use it on the unimportant notes—that is, on the central portion of the scale—but never on the important or closing notes. By this plan you give brilliance and color to the quick, passing notes leading up to the climax; then, by shutting the pedal off, the final and important notes ring out with an added value—clear, firm, and effective.

It would take a volume to tell all about the pedal, but these two things are the fundamental principles of its uses to work upon, and need a very careful application. Change the pedal with every change of harmony. In playing the lower notes on the keyboard its change should be still more frequent, because of the slow vibrations and the thickness of the tone in that part of the instrument.

The manner of holding the wrist should be individual, according to the need of the pupil, and must be decided by the teacher. Some play quick octaves and staccato passages by holding the wrist very high, while others employ a method exactly the opposite. Facility in octave-playing is not a matter of strength, for often players who have quick movement in octaves have not much strength. Of course, there are exceptions, such as Rubinstein, who had wrist fluency, lightness, and endurance.

One of the most important things in piano-playing is relaxation, thoroughly natural ease of attitude, and absolute absence of stiffness or rigidity in sitting at the instrument. Before the study of technique is begun, ease of attitude in the player must be fixed by the teacher. Poses and nervous movements cannot be too zealously guarded against. Many professionals might well practise before a mirror to observe themselves. The effect of even beautiful playing is spoiled by grimaces and restless bodily movements.

Only too many think that they display a vast deal of feeling if they make frequent *ritardandi* and long pauses on single notes. I would call this oversentimentalism simply the abuse of rhythm. The only way to avoid this is to keep as strictly as possible to the rhythm and the tempo. Nothing is to be gained by such affectation but distortion of the composer's ideas. Under this same head comes the exaggeration of the rubato, so deplorably frequent in the playing of Chopin. This springs from the same mistaken notion that it adds feeling and character. The only remedy of the fault is to stick closely to both rhythm and tempo.

I am a believer in discipline. As long as a student is enjoying the advice of a teacher he should follow his directions absolutely. Any one who would insist upon his own interpretation should not have a teacher. If he thus imposes upon the teacher, and he gives in, the loss is the student's. A teacher, of even a small reputation, represents a system, and it is of the greatest importance in any kind of work to have a system.

As technical studies I recommend Czerny's Opus 740, and Clementi's "Gradus ad Parnassum," the Tausig edition. The Czerny is pure technique, and the Clementi is extensive and brilliant. These, together with some special finger exercises by the teacher, suited to the individual need of the pupil, will, for a considerable time, be quite sufficient in the way of purely technical studies. Afterward the "Wohltemperirte Clavier" by Bach, indispensable in training the independence of the fingers and the tone, should be taken up, and in due course the studies by Chopin.

I do not believe in the clavier as a help to the student, because by it he loses the possibility of controlling his playing. Its help will be not for him, but for his neighbors—it will keep him from disturbing them.

It is only by playing the scales with strong accent, and the slower the better, that precision and independence of the fingers are acquired. First play the scale through, accenting the notes according to the natural rhythm. Then, as in speech, let the accent fall upon the weak note instead of upon the strong one, and play the scale, accenting every second note; afterward place the accent upon every third note, then upon every fourth. This gives absolute command of the fingers, and is the only way to acquire it.

The piano is so rich in literature for the student at every stage of his advancement that a book would be required to give a list of all the works open to selection. To give a partial catalogue would only mean to slight a vast number of works equally worthy of mention.

I shall confine myself to naming some composers, who, in the general run of study, would be of advantage to the student, and yet are neglected. First of all I should advise Mozart, because, with our modern nerves and excitement, it becomes difficult to play with calm and simplicity. And these are the qualities that are required by Mozart.

Of neglected older composers one of the greatest of them all is Mendelssohn, whose "Songs Without Words" are of such admirable use in acquiring a singing quality of tone, and whose style of writing for the piano is of the best. Then, too, for brilliancy of technique I should advise Weber.

For advanced pianists I would recommend the playing of Moszkowski among the modern composers. His compositions, from the pianistic and pedagogic point of view, are perfect, and it is my conviction that it is scarcely possible to imagine a more perfect "clavier Satz" than Moszkowski gives us.